Praise for the *Earth Spirit* series

There is no doubt that this world is in crisis. The ecological and sociological reality we're living in and must face up to is quite frankly terrifying. Yet there is hope. The authors of the *Earth Spirit* series from Moon Books show us that there are solutions to be found in ecological and eco-spiritual practices. I recommend this series to anyone who is concerned about our current situation and wants to find some hope in solutions they can practice for themselves.
Sarah Kerr, Pagan Federation President

This bold and rich *Earth Spirit* series provides vital information, perspectives, poetry and wisdom to guide and support through the complex environmental, climate and biodiversity challenges and crisis facing us all. Nothing is avoided within the wide range of author views, expertise and recommendations on eco-spirituality. I am deeply inspired by the common call, across the books, to radically change our relationship with the planet to a more respectful, mutual, spiritual and sustainable way of living; both individually and collectively. Each book offers its own particular flavour and practical offering of solutions and ways forward in these unprecedented times. Collectively the series provides an innovative, inspiring and compelling compendium of how to live, hope and act from both ancient and modern wisdoms. Whatever your views, concerns and aspirations for your life, and for the planet, you will find something of value. My life and understanding is deeply enhanced through the privilege of reading this series.
Dr Lynne Se~~domore~~ CBE, Founder of Goddess Luminary Leadership W~~...~~ ~~...~~tess and ex Chief Executive

In a world that is faced with such immense environmental issues, we can often feel paralysed and impotent. The *Earth Spirit* series is a welcome and inspiring antidote to fear and apathy. These books gift us with positive and inspiring visions that serve to empower and strengthen our own resolve to contribute to the healing of our planet, our communities and ourselves.

Eimear Burke, Chosen Chief of The Order of Bards, Ovates and Druids

Thanks to Moon Books and an amazing group of authors for stepping up in support of our need to address, with grace and aliveness, the ecological crises facing humanity. We must take concerted, focused, positive action on every front NOW, and this is best and most powerfully done when we base our offerings in a deep sense of spirit. White Buffalo Woman came to us 20 generations ago, reminding us of the importance of a holy perception of the world - based in Oneness, unity, honor and respect. Even as that is profound, it is also practical, giving us a baseline of power from which to give our gifts of stewardship and make our Earth walk a sacred one - for us and for All Our Relations. Walk in Beauty with these authors!

Brooke Medicine Eagle, Earthkeeper and author of *Buffalo Woman Comes Singing and The Last Ghost Dance*

Earth Spirit is an exciting and timely series. It has never been more important to engage with ideas that promote a positive move forward for our world. Our planet needs books like these - they offer us heartening signposts through the most challenging of times.

Philip Carr-Gomm, author of *Druid Mysteries, Druidcraft and Lessons in Magic*

Our relationship to the Mother Earth and remembering our roles as caretakers and guardians of this sacred planet is essential in weaving ourselves back into the tapestry of our own sacred nature. From the shamanic perspective, we are not separate from nature. The journey to finding solutions for the Earth will come through each person's reconnection to her heartbeat and life force.

Chandra Sun Eagle, author of *Looking Back on the Future*

This is important work as we humans face one of the greatest challenges in our collective history.

Ellen Evert Hopman, Archdruid of Tribe of the Oak and author of *A Legacy of Druids, A Druid's Herbal of Sacred Tree Medicine, The Sacred Herbs of Spring*, and other volumes

What people are saying about

Ancient Wisdom, Modern Hope

Insightful, wise, and timely. Jim Powers gives us a number of unique and crucial considerations that must become part of the conversation about global warming. Moving back in time and beyond the science, *Ancient Wisdom, Modern Hope* reveals ancient perspectives and essential solutions for stemming the tide of climate change, both individually and collectively. Well-written and researched, concise and crystal clear!

Jane B. Burns, OM Shamanic Practitioner, Celtic Reiki Master, Shamanic Teacher and Practitioner and author of *Up a Tree: A Novel and Shamanic Handbook*

In *Ancient Wisdom, Modern Hope* James Powers offers a blueprint for reconnecting with nature in ways that can help us both understand where we have come from and choose more wisely the direction in which we're headed. Leading the reader on a journey through the history of the native peoples of his beloved New England, Powers underscores the importance of an animistic worldview: the idea that plants, animals, and the Earth itself are inspirited beings worthy of reverence and respect. This is not a how-to book in the usual sense of starting projects or activities. Instead, it is one that invites the reader toward a change of heart and mind that will inform their decisions going forward toward a better world.

Laura Perry, author of *Ariadne's Thread*

Ancient Wisdom, Modern Hope is a fascinating and important look at the human relationship with the natural world across history and into the modern climate crisis. Focusing particularly on the Indigenous communities in Connecticut USA, the book nonetheless offers wider lessons on living with nature, the cost of capitalism, and how wisdom from native American cultures meshes with modern scientific knowledge and offers a possible way forward for us all. Truly vital reading.

Morgan Daimler, author of *Fairies: A Guide to the Celtic Fair Folk* and *A New Dictionary of Fairies*

James Powers writes a passionate exploration about our profound relationship to the environment throughout history and the importance of relearning the sustainable habits of the past so that we can thrive in the future. The earth and our spirits are intertwined, making it our divine responsibility to heal the environment and live in a way that enables us to live in harmony with all things. *Ancient Wisdom, Modern Hope* is a must-read book for the modern mystic looking to restore the balance between the earth and those who inhabit it.

Dr. Maria DeBlassie, author of *Everyday Enchantments*

Ancient Wisdom, Modern Hope clearly delineates the sustainability of the indigenous relationship with our Mother Earth as opposed to the modern individualist framework. This shift in perspective is a necessary component to creating long-term solutions to the climate crisis.

Hearth Moon Rising, author of *Divining with Animal Guides*

EARTH SPIRIT

Ancient Wisdom Modern Hope

Relearning Environmental Connectiveness

EARTH SPIRIT

Ancient Wisdom
Modern Hope

Relearning Environmental
Connectiveness

James T. Powers

**MOON
BOOKS**

Winchester, UK
Washington, USA

JOHN HUNT PUBLISHING

First published by Moon Books, 2021
Moon Books is an imprint of John Hunt Publishing Ltd., No. 3 East Street, Alresford
Hampshire SO24 9EE, UK
office@jhpbooks.net
www.johnhuntpublishing.com
www.moon-books.net

For distributor details and how to order please visit the 'Ordering' section on our website.

ISBN: 978 1 78279 244 4
978 1 78279 245 1 (ebook)
Library of Congress Control Number: 2021938946

Design: Matthew Greenfield

UK: Printed and bound by CPI Group (UK) Ltd, Croydon, CR0 4YY
Printed in North America by CPI GPS partners

Published in association Pagan Dawn, a Pagan Federation magazine.

We operate a distinctive and ethical publishing philosophy in
all areas of our business, from our global network of authors to
production and worldwide distribution.

Contents

Preface   1
Introduction: The Warning   3

Part One: Who We Were: The First People, their Environment, and a Living Earth   13

Chapter One: The First Five Thousand Years   15
Chapter Two: Adaptability and Survival   25
Chapter Three: The Archaic Transition   33
Chapter Four: The Disaster Begins   42

Part Two: Ancient Lessons for a Modern World   51
Chapter Five: A Second Chance   53
Chapter Six: Shifting Perceptions   64
Chapter Seven: Changing Consciousness   75
Chapter Eight: The Choice is Ours to Make   86

About the Author   93
End Notes   94
Bibliography   100

Previous Books by James T. Powers

Saving the Farm
A Journey Through Time, Place, and Redemption
ISBN:9781938846069

Seeing the Past
Stories on the Trail of a Yankee Millwright.
ISBN:9781938846861

On the Edge of Uncertainty
The Siege and Battles of Saybrook Fort During the Pequot War,
1636-1637.
Old Saybrook Historical Society

This book is dedicated to my wife Adriana who has shared countless conversations about the nature of spirit, consciousness, and our human connection to the world around us.

"A good way to start thinking about nature, talk about it. Rather talk to it, talk to the rivers, to the lakes, to the winds as to our relatives."

John (Fire) Lame Deer, Seeker of Visions

Preface

We all know that the Earth and all life on it is in danger. Even those who deny the fact that human actions have created the climate and environmental crisis threatening to overwhelm the planet recognize what is happening. With our sophisticated communication technology, we are privy to the news of catastrophic climate events that take place daily around the world, our nation, and even where we live. Powerful storms, tremendous floods, massive wildfires, extreme droughts, and deadly heatwaves have become the norm. Melting sea ice and glaciers in Greenland and Antarctica threaten coastal cities and communities worldwide as the level of the oceans rise. Forests are disappearing and desertification is spreading. Mass extinctions of plant and animal life is increasing. It is as if we are living in a dystopian future; the problem is that future is now, and it is of our own making.

It is clear the Earth is trying to get our attention yet, as most of us go about our daily lives, it is easier to ignore the frightening warnings than think about them, let alone face them. Like many, I have felt overwhelmed and powerless as the continuing ecological and biological disasters confronting the planet rapidly unfold. A late summer hike to an ancient rock shelter used for thousands of years by the Indigenous people who once inhabited the area where I live changed that.

I am a retired teacher; also an historian, archaeologist, and researcher who's mind and interests have always dwelled in the past in order to dig deeper into how, who we are as a people, has been shaped by our collective past. Part of that quest has been to study and research the lifeways and beliefs of those who came before us, in the case of this book, the Indigenous people of Southern New England. An important part of that understanding has been to learn how as a culture, they related

1

to the environment not just in a physical manner, for example, how they shaped and used it, but their spiritual connection to it and all aspects of the Living Earth.

This led me to travel back in time to the end of the Ice Age when the first human inhabitants of Connecticut arrived; the Paleo-Indians and the subsequent Archaic and Woodland cultures that thrived for a period of 14,000 years. What made the people of those cultures, despite dramatic environmental changes, so successful? How did they relate to their environment and view their role in it? The archaeological and historical record, modern Indigenous cultures, the growing Spiritual Ecology movement, and my own studies of Indigenous cultural beliefs began to shape answers to those questions. Coupled with my understanding of Indigenous and modern shamanic practices as well as research into the how our brain shapes the way we see the world and cultures, I was able to piece together an understanding of how the Indigenous people of the past and present were and are able to relate to and consciously live as part of an interconnected world in harmony with the Living Earth.

We can return to an ancient consciousness and perspective that allowed not just Indigenous people in the past, but all of our ancestors, to live in a sustainable, respectful and interdependent manner with all life on the planet. We can begin to heal our relationship with the Earth before it is too late. There is hope and the answer is simple; the wisdom of the past can guide us towards a better future.

James T. Powers
April 14, 2021

Introduction

The Warning

"I do not think the measure of a civilization is how tall its buildings of concrete are, but rather how well its people have learned to relate to their environment and fellow man."[1]
Sun Bear, Chippewa (1929-1992)

It was one of those gorgeous early September days we often have in Southern New England; blue sky flecked with high wispy clouds gently moving in the soft breeze, warm sunshine radiating through the canopy of the forest, and the late summer sounds of insects and katydids. As I entered the trail that would lead me to my destination, following the familiar path, it did not take me long to come across torn branches and uprooted trees; the legacy of a ferocious tropical storm followed by severe thunderstorms and micro-bursts that had battered the region a week later. Many of the hulking tree trunks and broken tops were scattered throughout the woods, forming obstacles to what was normally a relatively uneventful walk through a maturing second growth woodland. The power of nature I thought to myself as I climbed through a tangle of branches formed by a recently downed oak.

I am not a scientist. I am an historian, archaeologist, and teacher who has been spending long hours hiking the many trails that meander over the rocky, forested ridges that surround the small town where I live. But one thing has been brought home strikingly to me after I began these hikes since my retirement from teaching: there is no doubt that the environment of the area is rapidly changing and the hills and woodlands bear testimony to that fact. Warmer snowless winters, wetter than average springs, and oppressively hot and humid summers are taking their toll on the natural landscape of the region. It is an alarming and sad fact that our highly advanced technological civilization is causing what may be irreversible harm and long-term devastation to our environment and for the future inhabitants who will call this place home.

The results of a recent study co-authored by University of Connecticut researchers that was published in the journal *Nature* appeared in the September 2020 issue of *Connecticut Magazine*. The data starkly showed how the climate has evolved and where it is headed by 2050 and 2100. Here are the results:

- *Heat waves will double from an average of 4 per year currently to 8 by 2050.*
- *"Tropical Nights" (when temperatures stay above 68 degrees) will increase from 10 per year in the 1950's to 45 per year by 2050.*
- *The average temperature in winter has risen from 26 degrees in 1895 to 30 degrees now and will rise to 40+ degrees by 2100.*
- *Days when there is frost will decrease from 140 days in the 1950's to 80 by 2050 and 50 by 2100.*
- *There will be fewer days when the temperature stays at or below 32 degrees; 25 in the 1950's, 10 by 2050 and 5 by 2100.*
- *The Growing Season will expand from 240 days in the 1950's to 275 days by 2050 and 300+ days by 2100.*[2]

These changes will have a profound impact on every aspect of people's lives while changing the ecology of the region with a catastrophic loss of the biodiversity. It is a grim outlook.

Genesis 1:26 *Then God said, "Let us make man in our image, after our likeness. And let them have dominion over the fish of the sea and over the birds of the heavens and over the livestock and over all the earth and over every creeping thing that creeps on the earth."*

This has been part of the problem. It is not the Judeo-Christian ethos, spirituality, or religious practices themselves that are the problem; but the premise and perceptions created in regard to the basic relationship people have with all of nature and the planet itself. As Western Civilization has evolved over the last 2000 years, the magnitude of the impact of that relationship has dramatically increased. In our desire and drive to establish dominion over the planet we have proceeded to systematically destroy and alter the environment and climate that has sustained all life on Earth since we humans first began to transform our way of life with the advent of farming. The pace of that alteration has accelerated since the Industrial Revolution 200 plus years ago and has been propelled further with an explosion of change during the second half of the 20th century.

Since then, scientific, technological, and medical advances have created a materialistic world unimagined even 50 years ago. These advances have brought about a better material standard of living while bringing great wealth to some, poverty to many, and a profound alienation away from nature and the Living Earth that all life depends upon. At the same time scientific and climatic forecasts for the immediate and long-term future have become so frightening and traumatic, it is easier psychologically, emotionally, and intellectually to ignore them for most than confront their reality. But it does not need to be this way. Humanity knows the answer and has for thousands of years.

My recent walk in the woods is a metaphor for the climatic changes and extreme weather events taking place. As I began walking along the path that is part of a trail system that meanders through Connecticut and links up eventually with those of the rest of New England, everything seemed at first to be "normal". But anyone who spends a bit of time in the woods knows that there is no such thing as normal. Every day brings with it changes that can be observed. A woodland is ever changing; via the seasons, the weather, the sunlight, and through all the life forms that live within it. It is never the same from day-to-day, week-to-week, month-to-month, or year-to-year. For the occasional hiker, happy to escape from the treadmill of daily life and routines, the subtle changes may not be obvious as they relish and celebrate their chance to escape and be one with nature.

But on that day, despite the beauty of the sky, perfect temperature, and familiar trail, it became dramatically clear that a catastrophic event had taken place. Storms have always uprooted trees and will continue to do so; some fall simply by chance, some because they have shallow roots that cannot maintain a grip with the soil, and some because they have been weakened by disease or insect infestations. Within fifty yards into the hike I could see something was different. The forest floor on either side of the path was littered by trees great and small; oaks, birches, ash, hemlocks, and others. Some were large and magnificent specimens that looked like a giant had come through and plucked them from the ground and tossed them to the side like a gardener pulling weeds. Others were toppled and hung up on their sisters, forming great triangles of trunks while some leaned precariously waiting for the next strong breeze to send them to the ground.

Even more startling were entire top sections of mature and towering trees that were snapped or twisted off and lay blocking the trail or scattered across the forest floor. They looked like a giant and friends had come through, dead heading the tree tops like one would to dried and dead flower blossoms in a garden. But these were not dead tree tops, but full of green leaves that had been that tree's contribution to the canopy. Together with their uprooted companions, they formed the legacy of destruction brought to the woods by two unrelated yet powerful weather events.

As I continued along the trail as best I could, climbing over, under, and more often around the fallen, I felt a deep and profound sadness. Here lay innocent victims of climate change. There have always been occasional tropical storms and hurricanes to strike Connecticut along with ferocious nor'easters in the winter. The recent storm, contrary to forecasts, exploded in intensity over the state with powerful winds of far greater strength and duration than predicted. To the frustration and anger of many, damage to property was extensive and electrical power for some was knocked out for up to nine days. It was a reminder of the power of nature and that we highly technical humans are still powerless before it. When a ferocious line of thunderstorms roared through a little over a week later, spurring a tornado nearby and numerous micro-bursts of violent winds, those of us effected were humbled. And this forest suffered.

One of the documented results of the evolving climate crisis is that extreme weather events are becoming the new normal and a direct result of our human activities and negligence. The climate crisis though often dramatic in its manifestation, is for the most part subtle and at times even benevolent in the short-term. A longer growing season and warmer winters – who can argue with that? But it is the long-term damage done to the biodiversity and ecology of the region and the entire planet that has become obvious to even the most casual observer. Serious scientific research has spawned report after report warning of what is happening and why. But we as a species persist on finding it easier to ignore the proof than confront the grimly distressing future the warnings project. Awareness has begun to grow for some individuals, however, and simple choices are being made; buy more efficient light bulbs, recycle, and even switch to a hybrid vehicle. These changes are laudable; they make us feel we are doing our part, and are to be commended. Unfortunately, they are not enough. To go beyond and question the very foundations of our comfortable lifestyles and standard of living is a non-starter.

There needs to be a cultural change in perception in regard to the relationship we humans have with all life on the planet and the Earth as a whole. We must develop a reciprocal relationship that is based upon an understanding of the connectedness and interdependence of all life and that the Earth is an interconnected living organism. Indigenous people here and throughout the world have always known this as did our ancestors no matter where they once lived, whether Europe, Asia, Africa, or the Americas.

Cultural bias is our greatest roadblock to embracing their ancient and powerful understanding of how the Earth really works within its web of reciprocal dependency. Because the Judeo-Christian theology that underpins our culture and formed our world view has separated us humans from the rest of nature, we continue to proclaim and act on our domination over it. This coupled with the legacies of the Scientific and Industrial Revolutions, with their fact based and data driven approach towards all questions of life and existence, has moved us away from any sense or understanding of the vital connections we as humans have with the Living Earth. This mind set, together with our Western capitalist economic system that has swept around the entire world has resulted in our present exploitive, acquisitional, materialistic, and mechanistic view of the Earth and Universe. This world view has led to incredible technological and intellectual advances that have brought about the material advances our culture has benefited from and celebrates. But the end game of this view however has also been rampant consumerism and the over exploitation of natural resources needed to sustain the acquisition and accumulation of material goods which have become our culture's badge of success and identity. Any non-scientific, wholistic perception of the Living Earth, past or present, is rejected as simply superstition and a primitive metaphysical anachronism.

This is not a call to abandon the positive progress our culture has made in the realms of science, medicine, and technology, but rather a call to create a more stable and sustainable way of life that recognizes that we must change our relationship with the planet. The trajectory we are following world-wide, led by our Western example, cannot be sustained in its current form according to scientific research published in report after report released over the last thirty years.

As far back as 1992, a group of more than 1600 senior scientists that included a majority of Nobel Laureates published a document titled the "Warning to Humanity" through the auspices of the Union of Concerned Scientists. Their warning was straight forward and direct. The scientists said:

"A great change in our stewardship of the Earth and life on it is required, if vast human misery is to be avoided and our global home on this planet is not irretrievably mutilated".[3]

The warning was a blaring siren call to restore a belief in the reciprocity and connectiveness of life on the planet threatened to be lost as a result of humanity's blind rush to accumulate at the expense of future generations. Their warning, like so many others since, was ignored.

Fast forward to 2020 and the Union of Concerned Scientists is still sounding the alarm. On their website they warn:

"As the amount of carbon dioxide increases, the planet warms up. Sea levels rise. Extreme weather becomes more commonplace. A whole range of impacts – from wildfires, to flooding, to extreme heat and drought – become more likely and more severe". The scientists continue: *"If we do nothing, these impacts will worsen. Large swarths of the world's population will migrate. Entire island nations may disappear. The magnitude and range of impacts means that almost every human on Earth will be affected, if they're not already."*[4]

A study by climate scientists from across the globe of the patterns of changes in climate and its impact in 2019 is frightening. The World Meteorological Organization published their results of surveys of weather data for that year. Their report outlined the increase in greenhouse gases; carbon dioxide (147%), methane (259%), and nitrous oxide (123%) since the Pre-Industrial Era by 2018. These have resulted in a mean temperature rise since 1850 of 1.1degrees Celsius. They warned that at the current pace, temperatures will assuredly rise above those set by The United Nations and the international community during global conferences and the consequent agreements. The goal is to try and keep the increase by 2100 to 1.5 degrees (2.7 degrees Fahrenheit). Meanwhile sea level rise is assured through the unprecedented melting of sea ice and glaciers in Greenland and Antarctica.[5] The climate crisis is spinning out of control and clearly getting away from our ability to confront it or make changes to deal with it.

One of the arguments against climate change has been that weather is always changing and it is impossible to prove that human induced climate change exists. A relatively new field of climate study called "event attribution science" is now giving scientists the ability to measure the impact of climate change on increasingly extreme weather events. What scientists do is assess through simulations how weather systems would behave if the large amounts of carbon dioxide generated by human activity during the last two centuries had not been deposited into the atmosphere. The results clearly show that climate change is amplifying historical weather patterns that have existed using world-wide weather records from over the past 100+ years.[6] This explains why heatwaves, droughts, and storms are becoming more extreme.

So what can we do? We can begin to look at the Earth and all its living and nonliving parts in a different more interconnected, wholistic, ancient, and vital way. A mindset that regards all life forms and the inanimate elements within the environment as part of an incredibly beautiful, connected whole. Above all we must come to see that as humans, we are part of a Living Earth and that the choices we make will determine the future of the planet. If we do not, we will be doomed to repeat the tragic mistakes of the past that have led us to this point. This is the premise of this book.

Part One

Who We Were:

The First People, their Environment,
and a Living Earth

Chapter One

The First Five Thousand Years

*"And while I stood there I saw more than I can tell and I understood
more than I saw, for I was seeing in a sacred manner the shapes of all
shapes as they must all live together as one being."*[1]
Black Elk, Oglala Lakota Holy Man (1863-1950)

That morning, my hike brought me to a place I return to often.
Tucked into a woodland full of scattered stony ridges, rocks,
and great boulders dropped by the retreating glacier as the
Ice Age began to end 16,000 years ago, the trail zig zags up,
around, and over the warren of geological features making the
hike interesting, scenic, and at times a bit challenging. Once I
overcame the geological obstacles and those the storms left
behind, I was excited to discover that my destination was not
blocked by tangles of fallen branches or any of the trees that stand
like sentinels before it. It was clear of debris and open; unscathed
by the turbulence that had swirled around it. The familiar face
of stone stood timeless as always, an ancient monument to the
millions of Earth years she stood as a silent witness, forever
watching, forever knowing. Impervious to change she had but
one enemy who had the power to alter or destroy her.

Like the land around her, she was born during the Triassic
Period, between 237 and 201 million years ago, part of a
tremendous, long lasting, volcanic flow of molten lava that over
time formed into a stony bed as layer after layer cooled. As it
did, the layers of sediments and minerals became the solid rock
called basalt which makes up much of the bedrock throughout
this region of Connecticut. Far from being a flat surface, the
bedrock is broken and uneven, forming undulating ridges that
primarily run north to south with low valleys between them.

Scattered everywhere are rocky outcrops that appear to have risen magically from the ground around them. Each outcrop pulls you towards them, magnetically exuding an earthly energy in their call to be inspected. My destination, one of hundreds, is larger than most but smaller than others. Locally, she is known as Coginchaug Cave.

Over the centuries, water, wind, and ice had slowly whittled and gouged at her to shape her eastern face creating a jagged cliff; her upper half projecting out and over the lower one forming a large, rocky overhang that shields the soil on the surface, forming a natural but uneven floor at the cliff base. Her solid skin, warm to the touch in the summer sun and cold under winter clouds, is always changing as the seasons and light change. A closer look at her wall reveals the diversity of colors that make up her true character; multiple shades of gray running from noticeably light to almost black predominate. Within the grays are streaks and swaths of burnt amber, rusty brown, blue-green, yellow, and creamy white. Each color represents a separate volcanic mix of minerals that came with her birth. As animate life evolved following the retreat of the glacier, her pronounced overhang became a timeless place of refuge from sun, rain, and snow. She became a sheltering place, a rock shelter.

The glacier that entered Connecticut 26,000 years ago was the southern edge of the great Laurentide Ice Sheet that covered most of present-day Canada, New England, New York, and the Great Lakes region of the United States. The one-mile-thick Ice Sheet reached its maximum extent 20,000 years ago when its southern end formed a moraine of glacial deposits pushed before it like a plow creating Long Island. As the glacier moved south, it picked up broken rocks and sediment peeled off from the landscape, rounding off hills as it stripped the local basalt ridges and valleys between bare. This southward movement often "plucked" large sections of those basalt ridges off on their southern side resulting in the jagged cliffs and rock shelters found throughout the area.

When the process of melting increased 16,000 years ago, the Ice Sheet began to slowly retreat north leaving in its wake the rock-strewn topography that exists today.

As the glacier began its northward trek, all of Connecticut except for the southeastern section was still covered by the Ice Sheet. There was no Long Island Sound and the mainland extended approximately sixty miles south of Long Island onto the Continental Shelf. A fresh water lake formed where Long Island Sound is today and other smaller glacial lakes and ponds were created by glacial melt water as the Ice Sheet moved north. The land quickly sprang to life in the form of a cold arctic tundra filled with mosses, grasses and other types of low growing plants and woody shrubs that typify that treeless ecosystem. The short growing season attracted migrating Ice Age animals such as mastodon, mammoths, and caribou. Other extinct creatures, among them dire wolves, saber toothed tigers, four horned antelope, and giant beaver arrived. Into this environment around 14,000 years ago, came another seasonal migrant; small groups of Paleo-Indians who followed the migrating herds; the first people to arrive in Connecticut. Finding shelter in this harsh environment was a matter of survival which drew them instinctively to the many rock shelters scattered throughout the region.

These earliest Paleo-Indians traveled in small family groups of 20 to 50 individuals as they foraged and hunted while following the herds of migrating animals. Acutely attuned to their environment in ways we can only imagine, their very existence and survival depended upon their intimate understanding of and relationship with every living and non-living thing around them. Their nomadic lifeway led them to establish both temporary open-air campsites building shelters that could be quickly dismantled as they moved, while often utilizing rocky outcrops such as Coginchaug Cave as shelters. By 13,000 years ago the climate began to warm as the glacier retreated farther into Northern New England and the tundra was replaced by a mixed boreal forest of spruce, pine, birch, and oak. The changing climate and ecology allowed the Paleo-Indians to remain in the area longer, eventually permanently, while maintaining seasonal migrations to take advantage of foraging and hunting opportunities. This would have led to an increased use of rock shelters as residential sites, especially in the winter.

Rock shelters, unlike caves, by their very nature are partly open despite the overhanging top section which would have provided some protection from the rain, snow, and wind. To compensate for the opening and provide a drier and warmer space within the shelter, a frame of long poles would have been placed at an angle from the ground to the upper face of the rock and skins would have been draped across the wooden frame. This would have provided a dry area protected from the weather for the family group. Ideally, a rock shelter would have been chosen, especially in the winter, if it faced east or southeast to take advantage of the warmth of the morning sun. Inside, a fire or fires would heat the air and the rock wall creating a comfortable and inviting space. Undoubtedly this would have been true of Coginchaug Cave as its size, inclination of the overhang, and eastern orientation would have made it a desirable location to shelter from the weather. There are numerous places on the stony ceiling of the overhang where smokey discoloration can be seen though it is all but impossible to tell when the fires that left their mark might have been lit over the thousands of years people have visited the shelter.

A location near a water source was also critical and each documented shelter used by Paleo-Indians in Connecticut are located near a river, stream, pond, or lake. Coginchaug Cave looks across a small valley of maybe 150 yards in width to another rocky ridge. Together they work to provide a degree of protection from the wind. Both outcrops form a barrier that diverts a strong breeze away from the shelter as I recently witnessed when I saw the lack of tree damage from the recent storms that tore through the area. In the valley formed between the shelter and her sister ridge is a stream that runs parallel to the two outcrops. During the period of glacial melting, the tremendous volume of water flowing between the two ridges would have helped to shape the valley and the shelter. When Paleo-Indians arrived and occupied the area the stream would have been considerably larger in size and water volume as it made its way northwest towards what was once a glacial lake called Lake Middletown. The lake bed is now an extensive wetland known as the Coginchaug Swamp.

A study of known Paleo-Indian sites published in the *Archaeological Society of Connecticut Bulletin* (2014 v.76) by Michael C. Bouchard listed seven rock shelters that had been professionally excavated in Connecticut where stone artifacts such as projectile points and scrapers were found associated with Paleo-Indians. The shelters were among 72 known Paleo-Indian sites and encampments distributed throughout the state.[2] Coginchaug Cave is not among them. No artifacts have been reported to have been found there which is typical of known Native sites that have been visited and disturbed by artifact collectors for hundreds of years. Any artifacts associated with Paleo-Indian or later Indigenous inhabitants disappeared long ago.

So who were these people and what was their relationship to the environment? The first thing to understand is that the amount of time Paleo-Indians lived in Connecticut and the region was approximately 5,000 years (14,000 to 9,000 years ago), by far the longest existing time period of any other culture. During those 5,000 years, Paleo-Indian people were resilient in their ability to repeatedly adapt to the most radical and dramatic climatic and environmental changes to have taken place since humans first arrived in North America during the Ice Age. Having entered Connecticut in the wake of the retreating glacier, they were able to respond to environmental changes brought by changing climate conditions by developing adaptive strategies that allowed them to not only survive, but prosper. This ability to adapt was due to their intimate knowledge and understanding of the environment in which they lived. They understood their interconnection to every aspect of their world and this understanding allowed them to work with their environment and not against it. Consequently, Paleo-Indians developed technologies and utilized surrounding resources available to them to successfully maintain their way of life for thousands of years.

Although it is impossible to ever really know exactly how Paleo-Indian people related to their environment and what their cosmological beliefs and spirituality may have included, it is fair to assume that they practiced a form of what today would be broadly classified as animism. Animism is an ancient world view that was practiced throughout Europe, Asia, Africa, Americas, and Australia before the advent of organized religions that coincided with the development of agriculture and state structures. It was practiced by Indigenous Americans prior to European contact and most certainly by Paleo-Indians. Animism forms the belief system for many Native Americans today and is still practiced by Indigenous people world-wide. At its core, animism understands that all created things have a life force, energy, or spirit that is conscious and it is possible to communicate with. This includes not just humans, but animals and plants. It also includes all things that make up the landscape such as rivers, lakes, and mountains, the elements such as rain and wind, and even the seasons. Through a reverence for all of creation, both animate and inanimate, according to animism, it is possible to communicate with every living and nonliving being and thing on the planet, even the Earth itself by tapping into and recognizing the unique life force or spiritual energy of each.

It is easy to dismiss an animist world view as primitive superstition when looked at through the lens of our sophisticated technologically advanced and scientific based culture. Yet animism has been the longest functional and successful belief system humans have practiced in order to relate to and learn from nature and prosper within their environment. For hundreds of thousands of years people have understood that their lives were interconnected with all living and non-living things and that reality made survival possible. Humans have always perceived and constructed a reality in which they live in order to survive and function within their particular culture which is tied to the environment where they live. This process, called environmental determinism, continues to play a role in shaping how a particular culture, even ours, adapts to and functions within its particular environment based upon existing geological and climatic factors.

The understanding and belief that humans have a deep spiritual connection to every aspect of the environment and that we have a reciprocal responsibility has until relatively recently in human history been the key to humanity's successful survival. The perception that all creation is interconnected changes not only how we view nature and everything within the surrounding environment, but how we interact within it. Our ancient ancestors, no matter where they lived on the planet, understood that their environment held the power of life and death over them. Therefore the communication of nature's messages and the ability to understand them was essential for survival.

Armed with this highly developed understanding of their connection with all living and nonliving things, Paleo-Indian people thrived for thousands of years within and even through a series of environmental and climatic changes our modern culture might very well find impossible to navigate. Of course our current culture is much more sophisticated and technologically advanced when compared to the materially primitive, nomadic Paleo-Indian culture and the idea of returning to such a primitive way of life without access to all the advances created by our civilization is impractical, impossible, and completely out of the question. But what is of crucial importance for our society at this point and time is a change of perception. The understanding of how we are all connected within the web of life on the planet is the message they are sending us. It is a message we cannot ignore. To continue to do so is already creating serious and devastating consequences for all life on Earth.

So how exactly did Paleo-Indian people function within their environment? Clearly, from 14,000 until 9,000 years ago when their culture evolved into the Archaic culture, these first people were familiar with strategies that lent to their survival in an extremely harsh and hostile world. The small groups of men and women who first followed the migrating caribou herds into Connecticut were fully experienced in the practical and spiritual ways of living necessary to navigate within the environment of their new home. They were following lifeways passed down to them by generation after generation of nomadic hunting and gathering ancestors who had first crossed into North America from Siberia and then travelled eastward across the continent to the current Northeastern U.S.

What they found was a land shaped by the retreating Ice Sheet that had given birth to a wild and unforgiving tundra that sustained the animals they depended upon for survival. Archaeologists believe they arrived in two waves over a period of time, migrating below the Ice Sheet along the northern coast of Glacial Lake Connecticut from what is now New York and New Jersey. This fresh water lake was located where Long Island Sound is today. These migrants eventually populated the western half of Connecticut. At the same time, migrant groups travelled along the southern coast of the lake to Long Island and the Continental Shelf to its south. Sixty miles of the Shelf was dry land since the Ice Sheet had absorbed incredible amounts of water from the ocean resulting in a tremendous drop in the level of the Atlantic Ocean. Unfortunately, many Paleo-Indian encampment sites are today under the Atlantic and even Long Island Sound. Once the sea level began to rise, the Continental

Shelf was reclaimed by the ocean and Glacial Lake Connecticut was submerged to become Long Island Sound.[3]

A second wave of migrants entered central and eastern Connecticut via the north from Massachusetts as the Ice Sheet continued to melt and retreat northward opening that migration route. These migrants probably entered the region through the Hudson River Valley and Western Massachusetts before turning south into Connecticut. Among these migrants were possibly the first to set eyes on Coginchaug Cave. Another large glacial lake had formed from glacial melt water in today's Connecticut River Valley 15,000 years ago as the Ice Sheet continued its slow retreat north into Vermont and New Hampshire. Nestled between the western and eastern highlands of Connecticut, Glacial Lake Hitchcock extended from Rocky Hill, Connecticut north into Vermont. For some unknown reason, the terminal moraine at Rocky Hill that held the lake in place burst 3,000 years later and the lake drained resulting in the formation of the Connecticut River and its valley. Until that time, archaeologists believe the lake had been a substantial east-west barrier for the migrating animals and people.[4]

Like all human cultures, the Paleo-Indians became successful because of their ability to exploit the resources they found around them. As nomadic hunters and gatherers, they moved with the herds seasonally and while in a specific area foraged and gathered edible plants, while fishing and hunting. According to archaeologists who have studied Paleo-Indian migration patterns, the arrival of people into Connecticut was probably not a haphazard wandering that by chance brought them here. People have rarely, even to this day, migrated voluntarily to a new location they know nothing about, especially when it is a family group contemplating a move.[5]

Archaeological evidence indicates one or two general scenarios; a pioneering process or a planned migration of either short or long distance. The pioneering process involved a scouting party that would have struck out into unfamiliar territory to ascertain its viability in terms of terrain, resources, and climate. Once convinced the new area was desirable, the larger group would then have begun the migration. A second pioneering process was through contact with people who would have had firsthand knowledge of the new destination and what it might offer the migrants. This implied movement to and from the region as well as contact through trade networks.

A planned short distance migration would have taken place once a new destination was identified. This would have entailed the group moving forward into a new location based upon available subsistence resources. The group would remain until the resources were depleted and then move on. Long distance migration would have proceeded in much the same manner as the short distance migration pattern except a predetermined destination would have required a longer distance to travel before reaching the ultimate goal. This form of movement would have taken place at a relatively rapid pace along natural corridors such as river valleys or coastlines that were already known.[6] Apparently all these forms took place during the thousands of overlapping years of Paleo-Indian presence in Connecticut.

Chapter Two

Adaptability and Survival

"Humankind has not woven the web of life. We are but one thread within it. Whatever we do to the web, we do to ourselves. All things are bound together. All things connect."[1]
Chief Seattle, Suquamish (1786-1866)

Human beings have always responded to the challenges of changes in their environment or climate by using adaptive strategies based upon the conditions that are present. Those conditions strongly influence land use and technological developments that enhance and make possible a way of life and the maintenance of a culture. Therefore, as climate and the ecology around a particular culture change, how the culture responds to those changes dictates the trajectory of their future course. A static reaction to evolving conditions will certainly bring about negative consequences. This is a basic law of nature. Animals, plant species, fish, birds, and insects all react to and respond to environmental change by seeking ways to adapt. They will often retract or expand their range or move to a different location depending on environmental conditions and stresses. Changes in the environment will also lead to an increase or decrease in their populations. If adaptation does not succeed, extinction is a distinct possibility.[2] There are no longer mammoths and mastodons in Connecticut.

The first Paleo-Indian people to enter the tundra environment of the region were certainly aware that they were entering a place that had not been frequented by their fellow humans to any great extent if at all. This likely gave them an initial advantage when it came to operating within this new environment. Animals not initially familiar with the threat humans might offer gave these early arrivals an advantage that more than likely evaporated quickly as the game they pursued adapted to the new predator. Over time, prey developed strategies that focused on survival while the hunters developed strategies to improve positive hunting outcomes.

According to archaeologists, paleontologists, and paleobotanists, prior to 11,000 years ago, North America was what could be called a "super Serengeti" with more big game species here than found in Africa today. The list is impressive: mammoths, mastodons, horses, tapirs, ground sloths, bears, giant jaguars, llama, antelope, bison, peccaries, giant beaver, dire wolves, saber toothed tigers, deer, and giant armadillos.[3] Many of these animals certainly were found in Connecticut when the first humans expanded their range into the region as the animals took advantage of the vegetation found during the short tundra growing season with the retreat of the glacier.

A period of mass extinction began in North America around 45,000 years ago with the expansion of the Laurentide Ice Sheet as the colder change in climate caused many of the types of vegetation the large herbivores depended upon to disappear. Over time remaining populations stabilized until the period of extinction greatly accelerated between 12,000 and 11,000 years ago due to the dramatically warming climate. As the Ice Sheet continued its movement north into Canada, ocean levels rose rapidly swallowing the open Continental Shelf and Long Island Sound.[4] What caused this sudden shift in climate?

Climatologists have studied this climate phenomena for years and have concluded that the Global Ice Sheets across Asia, Europe, and North America reached their greatest extent around 20,000 years ago when their advance stopped and the melting process began. As the glaciers melted, tremendous amounts of freshwater poured into the North Atlantic, raising its level as much as thirty meters in a few hundred years. This huge infusion of cold water apparently shut down the circulation of warm ocean currents moving north from the equatorial regions heating the oceans there. This changed the circulation of global wind currents bringing warmer air to the north and for reasons still not completely understood, the southern ocean regions began to release large concentrations of carbon dioxide as they heated. This release was approximately equivalent to the amount of carbon dioxide generated by human activities over the past 200 years. With the increase in carbon dioxide, the planet began to warm as energy from the sun became trapped in the atmosphere resulting in the relatively stable climate that has allowed humanity to thrive during the last 10,000 years by creating the environmental conditions that have made the development of civilization across the world possible.[5]

But what caused the Global Ice Sheets to halt their advance? It is understood that the Earth's orbit in relation to the sun changes over a period of thousands of years and that change or wobble has caused numerous Ice Ages (there have been 8 over the last 800,000 years) as well as the end of each by introducing a warmer Interglacial Period. The current Interglacial Period began 20,000 years ago. The orbital wobbles result in a greater or lesser amount of sunlight striking the northern latitudes of the planet. Less sunlight enhanced the growth of ice at the poles, more sunlight, periods of melting.

Climatologists also have theorized that the Ice Sheets by 20,000 years ago had literally reached their maximum size and extent possible and became unstable as they moved into lower latitudes where sunlight was stronger. This precipitated the melting process. In terms of geological time, the glaciers retreated rapidly ushering in a dramatic evolution in the ecology and climate of the Northeastern region of the United States and Canada.[6] Whatever the exact cause of the end of the last Ice Age was, the Paleo-Indian residents of Connecticut were able to adapt to the evolving environmental and ecological changes around them. However, it is extremely important to point out that the changes to the climate and ecology of the region took place continually over thousands of years leaving people ample time to adjust unlike the situation facing humanity today in which scientists and climatologists warn there are literally only a few decades to act to avoid a planetary catastrophe.

Prior to 12,000 years ago when the period of rapid warming began, the Paleo-Indian residents of Connecticut were well adapted to the tundra-like environment according to archaeologists who have studied and researched their lifeways based upon the scant evidence available. The 72 known Paleo-Indian sites are mostly temporary, single use occupation locations supporting the understanding that they lived a highly mobile existence in relatively small family groups as they foraged and hunted. Living in an environment comparable to that found today in the far northern latitudes of Canada, Alaska, and Siberia, they took advantage of every opportunity to provide for their survival. They were intimately connected to their environment and able to live comfortably and prosper in a cold, harsh climate. Proof of their existence at the known occupation sites has been predominantly through stone tool diagnostics. Archaeologists have been able to date the sites through projectile point styles that evolved over time in terms of shape, material, and size as changes in the environment brought about the need to adapt new technologies. Modern carbon dating techniques of charcoal from their fires as well as analysis of the seeds and animal bones from food consumed have opened windows into better understanding Paleo-Indian diet and the changing ecology over time.[7]

By 12,000 years ago, as the region continued to warm the vegetation of the tundra began to give way to different types of grasses and woody plants such as spruce, pine, alder, and birches. This had a significant effect on the megafauna, the large herbivores such as the mammoth and mastodon. The climate was still cool but warming, with an increase in moisture that allowed new plant species to migrate into the area. By 11,000 years ago the warming trend had accelerated the change in the ecological landscape even further by introducing trees such as hemlock and oak that replaced the earlier woody shrubs the large animals depended upon for their diet.[8]

For many years it was assumed that pressure from Paleo-Indian hunting was primarily responsible for the disappearance of animals such as the mammoth. Clearly, they may have had an impact as evidenced by a mastodon skeleton excavated in New York state accompanied by Paleo-Indian stone tools and projectiles. However, new research has shown that the most significant reason for the demise and extinction of the megafauna was their inability to digest the plants available to them as the ecology around them changed. It turns out that both mammoths and mastodons had a digestive system exclusively suited for the soft shoots of certain woody plants and grasses. The warmer climate replaced their food sources with newer types of vegetation that proved to be poisonous to them. Human hunting may have been a contributing factor bringing about their extinction, but not a significant one.

Proof of the changing environment after 11,000 years ago has come through the analysis of burned wood from Paleo-Indian camp fires. The charcoal often came from new species of trees that included oaks, other deciduous types, and conifers such as hemlock. As the warming continued over time, the entire ecological landscape was transformed becoming mostly forested with the addition of sugar maples, red maples, and chestnut.[9] With these changes the megafauna disappeared and were replaced by other species that thrived in the warmer, moist, and forested environment. Moose and elk were found alongside caribou requiring new strategies and technologies for hunting.

The standard projectile point utilized by Paleo-Indian hunters was a type called a fluted point.[10] This stone point had a shallow fluted section removed from the center of its base to allow it to be better attached to a spear shaft. Hunters utilized spears in one of two ways while hunting; stabbing or throwing it like a javelin. In both cases, a hunter was required to get close to his prey to maximize the use and force of the spear, a dangerous moment for any hunter. As a result, Paleo-Indian hunters utilized cooperative strategies when closing in on the animal as together they would force their prey into swamps where they would become stuck in the boggy muck, drive them off cliffs, or create traps and snares.

Towards the end of the Paleo-Indian period of occupation in Connecticut a new weapon was introduced that was better suited to hunting in the changing environment around 10,000 years ago; the atlatl.[11] This new weapon technology is reflected in the evolution of projectile point styles and the disappearance of the older fluted points. These new stone points were much smaller, slenderer, and non-fluted in order to fit on the end of a slender and lighter spear shaft that was typical of the atlatl. This new technology revolutionized hunting transforming the lifeways of the period by making an individual hunter more efficient. Projectile points during the entire Paleo-Indian period had come predominantly from locally available stone, most often quartz, but more exotic types from outside the region such as jasper and chert have been found at sites associated with Paleo-Indians. The lack of a local source for those stone types strongly indicates that the Paleo-Indian residents of Connecticut either travelled to quarry locations elsewhere or were part of a trade network connecting them to other groups outside the area.[12]

The atlatl, an Aztec word for the weapon, was utilized during the Paleo-Indian period and after throughout North America. Essentially a spear thrower, the atlatl consisted of a straight throwing stick about two feet long with a hook or notch on one end. The spear, approximately five to six feet in length and lighter and thinner than the heavier form used earlier, had its end place against the hooked end of the throwing stick while the shaft rested on the stick. A projectile point was attached to the other end of the shaft or a removable dart on a short hollowed out wooden shaft was inserted on the end. The dart technology allowed a hunter to retrieve the spear after the dart struck the prey, the force of the spear hitting the animal would eject the shaft allowing the hunter to retrieve it and reload another dart if needed. Because the throwing stick functioned as an extension of the hunter's arm, the spear could travel through the air with a much greater velocity and farther than a spear thrown by hand; up to 300 feet.

From the archaeological record established to date, most Paleo-Indian period occupation sites tend to be concentrated around inland lakes, swamps, and streams as opposed to major river valleys and flood plains or the coast. Reconstruction of the environment and ecology of the time has shown that as the post-glacial era proceeded, the river valleys were dangerously and often violently flooded and not conducive to settlement. Filled with fast flowing glacial meltwater, the river flood plains were frequently scoured of plant life and the pools left behind must have been breeding grounds for tremendous swarms of insects in warmer weather making them unsuitable for settlement. Without the accompanying wetlands and swamps of our present slower moving rivers, the plant, fish, and animal diversity would have been limited.[13]

The coastline was retreating under pressure from rapid sea level rise without the stabilizing benefit of marshes that typify much of this area today. The sea rise, estimated to have risen 30 meters (98.5 feet) in a few hundred years, reshaped the coastline and left in its wake isolated rocky islands often barren of vegetation and extensive mudflats all but impossible to travel across. Access to Long Island, previously blocked by Glacial Lake Connecticut, would have been even more difficult as the Atlantic poured in to create Long Island Sound.

As a result, Paleo-Indian groups sought more stable and thus safer locations away from those harsher environments to secure the resources needed to live. These upland and inland sites produced a greater number of plants, berries, nuts, and tubers to gather along with animals and birds to hunt and trap. The waters of lakes and ponds were filled with fish to catch. This does not mean that Paleo-Indian people avoided the river valleys or coast when foraging or hunting as they also offered a wide range of food resources; a great variety of fish, mollusks, various species of fowl and marine animals like seals. Yet navigating the dramatic climatic and ecological changes that transformed their environment required an inherent cultural adaptability based upon a keen knowledge of the world in which they lived as the landscape and weather changed around them. Those changes brought with them a completely new set of floral, faunal, and aquatic life they had to depend on.[14]

Understanding the habits and behaviors of the animals around them was critical to hunting success and like later hunter and gathering cultures developed a spiritual and respectful relationship with their prey. This included a deep knowledge and understanding of the plant life around them as well as the ability to read signs within nature and the weather. Of course we will never know exactly what the Paleo-Indian people knew, believed, and practiced including what their spiritual cosmology included. But based upon anthropological studies of Indigenous cultures from around the globe and historically documented Native American cultures past and present it is possible to speculate what it might have been.

Chapter Three

The Archaic Transition

"Every seed has awakened and so has all animal life. It is through this mysterious power that we too have our being and we therefore yield to our neighbors, even our animal neighbors, the same right as ourselves to inhabit this land."[1]
Sitting Bull, Hunkpapa Lakota (1831-1890)

Rising sea levels swamping low lying coastal regions, dramatically warming temperatures bringing about a radical transformation of the ecology and biodiversity of the environment through mass extinctions of faunal and floral life. All caused by tremendous amounts of carbon dioxide entering the atmosphere within a relatively short period of a few hundred years. Although this is a forecast for the near future of our planet, by looking to the past we can learn that our ancestors here also experienced the same environmental disruptions and changes. The difference is we have the ability to avoid such catastrophic changes they did not. Their ability to adapt was the key to their survival. Will it be the same for us?

By 9,000 years ago, the post glacial period had ended but a period of warming continued to transform the environment of Southern New England. This warming trend accelerated but fluctuated during the centuries that followed until approximately 4,000 years ago. In order to meet the demands of the changing climate and environment around them, the resident Paleo-Indians continued to adapt to the changes as their culture evolved to meet the new challenges.[2]

The climatic changes transformed the forests in the region as white pines and birches joined the already established oaks and hemlocks. Temperatures were on average much hotter in summers than present and winters much colder, requiring residents to adapt to the extreme differences in weather conditions.[3] Animals in the region became those that are recognizable today. White tailed deer, moose, and elk became the preferred prey and a mainstay of the diet as the culture evolved into a period archaeology identifies as Archaic. This Archaic Period lasted from around 9,000 years ago to roughly 3,000 years ago and is divided into four distinct cultural periods based upon adaptation to the changes in the environment as evidenced by changes in stone tool and projectile technology and types as well as diet; Early, Middle, Late, and Terminal.

Like the Paleo-Indian culture, most of what is known about life during the phases of the Archaic period come from archaeological investigations. Stone tool and projectile point diagnostics along with charcoal, seeds, and animal bones found in fire pits from the sites excavated have opened a window into their lifeways. Unlike known Paleo-Indian locations, there are many more Archaic sites indicating an overall increase in population. Undoubtedly, the transition to a warmer and more stable climate during the period allowed for a greater availability of resources promoting population growth. Most of the Archaic sites during the Early and Middle periods (9,000 to 6,000 years ago) are small, temporary sites used by small family groups or hunting parties. Many however, appear to have been used repeatedly over time indicating seasonal migrations to take advantage of food sources available.[4]

Beginning around 7,500 years ago and lasting until 5,000 years ago, a very warm and dry climatic period took hold of the region with its consequent dramatic impact on the ecological makeup of the environment. Archaeological evidence of the number of Archaic occupation sites dropped significantly indicating a reduction in the size of the population in Connecticut and the rest of Southern New England. There also appears to have been a shift in types of site locations from inland lakes and wetlands to river valleys and adjacent terraces as the traditional habitats utilized by earlier residents shrank or completely dried up.[5] Once again, adaptation was the key to survival. Animals previously depended upon for food and as a tool and clothing resources such as moose and elk moved north to colder climates just as the caribou had done earlier leaving the white-tailed deer as the primary prey.[6] This shift is seen in the changes in projectile point technology since hunting strategies and techniques evolved with the change in prey.

Towards the end of the Middle Archaic period a second type of projectile technology appeared in Connecticut apparently introduced from the Mid-Atlantic coastal region. This arrival also seems to coincide with an increase in occupation sites where the newer technology, termed a bifurcate point, replaced the older bifacial technology.[7] Did the new arrivals replace the older Archaic residents who had suffered population loss at the time due to the ecological and climate changes or did the older residents adopt the newer cultural technology? It was probably a combination of both.

This warm, dry, Middle Archaic period saw once again significant fluctuations in temperatures as the landscape continued to change. As the wetlands that had typified the earlier period shrank or dried up, forests retreated, and grasslands expanded. There was also a general transition to more drought resistant plants. The changes in the environment resulted in the Archaic people abandoning the earlier more permanent camp sites from which they would send out hunting and gathering groups to a more seasonal migration pattern within a particular territory. In this way, people were able to maximize their acquisition of food and other resources while establishing seasonal village locations. The most productive locations for the Middle Archaic villages have been found to be along rivers and the coast. These locations assured the most consistent seasonal food supply. A significant reliance on fish species, both anadromous and salt water is evidenced from archaeological investigations of known village and camp sites.[8]

As the climate began to stabilize towards the end of the Middle Archaic period, the environment contained a growing diversity of plant and animal species similar to that found in the region when the European contact period began roughly 400 years ago.[9] This growing diversity created an increased availability and abundance of food sources that triggered a substantial increase in the population. The archaeological record indicates that the people of that period had developed a highly successful relationship with the environment as they took advantage of the bounty each season offered within the territory where they lived. Excavation of their cooking hearths reveal a broad array of food types; white tailed deer, bear, racoon, squirrel, rabbit, turkey, water fowl, fresh and salt water fish, shell fish, snakes, and turtles. A long list of wild plants also made up a substantial part of their diet along with nuts and berries in season. The result was a well-balanced and nutritious diet that contributed to both good health and population growth.[10]

By relying on an intimate relationship with everything within their environment, the residents of the latter years of the Archaic period were able to take advantage of the biological and ecological diversity it offered. Undoubtedly part of that relationship was a strong spiritual connection to every living and non-living thing that surrounded them. All indications are that they viewed all within their environment within a context of reciprocity and gratitude. We will never know this for sure but this world view and belief system that prizes and respects the interconnectedness of all living and non-living things still existed within the Indigenous culture at the time of the arrival of Europeans into the region. There is a strong likelihood that this all-encompassing view and understanding of the world had been cultivated and passed down over the centuries allowing each successive generation to survive and thrive within the environment. Anthropologists have long understood that cultures like those that existed in much of the Americas prior to the arrival of Europeans practiced the world view that revolved around the simple belief that everything that existed on the earth was connected in a web of energy and existence that made all life possible in a cycle of cooperation and interdependence.

By the end of the Archaic Period and the start of the Woodland Period (around 3000 years ago), the climate and ecology of the region had stabilized into what was essentially our modern conditions although a bit wetter and cooler than the one that existed well into the 20th century before the present global climate began to profoundly change. The culture featured stable communities that utilized all the seasonal resources and locations across the environment with large multi seasonal camps or villages while establishing smaller task specific camps that often-utilized rock shelters.[11] Like their ancestors, settlement patterns continued to concentrate along river flood plains and the coast which held the most abundant food resources. During this period, the innovation of clay pottery was introduced through trade with people in the mid-Atlantic region resulting in a revolution in food processing that led to an increase in population.[12]

This early Woodland Period however was severely impacted by a brief climate anomaly that resulted in a cooling period known as the Little Ice Age.[13] Although it lasted only around 100 years, it had a profound impact on the ecology causing a decline in nut bearing plants and trees such as oaks. This resulted in a decline in the number deer and turkeys previously relied upon for food with a corresponding drop in the human population that had been increasing up to that point. This population collapse has been noted by the decline in the number of occupation sites found that date to this period. Yet once again, the people of the region were faced with adapting to the new environment; in this case concentrating in larger villages and camps along river and coastal locations, especially those close to marshlands to exploit the abundant year-round food resources found there.

By this time, Archaic/Woodland Period people were leaving behind expressions of spirituality and a belief in an afterlife that have been identified by archaeologists. Numerous cremation burials have been found which include grave goods, items from everyday life such as tools, cooking utensils, pottery, projectile points, and knives.[14] These were meant to be used by the deceased in the afterlife. Along with these items and at camp and village sites, smoking pipes have also been found.[15] The pipes would have been used in the ritualistic smoking of tobacco in ceremonies in which the tobacco smoke would carry the intent and prayers of the participants to the spirit world. This practice continued up into the time of European occupation of New England and is still practiced today. The sacred smoke of tobacco connected participants ritualistically to the world of the spirits and was an important metaphoric device utilized during religious, political, and curing ceremonies. It was believed to produce positive thoughts, cement friendships, and summon helping spirits while driving out evil ones.

Once the Little Ice Age ended, the climate of the region again stabilized leading to another period of population growth in the settlements along the river valleys and their associated uplands as well as in the coastal plain. Two important innovations and adaptations helped to spur this time of growth; the introduction of the bow and arrow 1,400 years ago and horticulture around 1,000 years ago.[16] Both were introduced, like clay pottery, through trade networks with residents in the Mid-Atlantic region.

The bow and arrow quickly replaced the atlatl; the smaller size of the arrows compared to the longer shaft holding the projectile point of the atlatl made it less cumbersome and its use more efficient. This coupled with an improvement in accuracy, distance and penetrating power revolutionized hunting making the ability to obtain meat and its needed protein easier thus improving the diet. However, as important an adaptation as the bow and arrow was, the introduction of horticulture proved to be the most transformative. Indigenous people going back to the time of the Paleo-Indians had depended on the seasonal availability of wild plants as a major if not the most important source of food. Wild plants still played an important role in the diet of Woodland culture but as time proceeded, they became increasingly supplemental to the Three Sisters; maize, beans, and squash.[17]

How the people of the Woodland Culture planted and viewed the Three Sisters is a great metaphor for their understanding of how their environment, the plants, and their relationship with them worked interdependently. Unlike the European colonists who practiced monoculture, the Indigenous people sowed the sisters in a way that allowed them to work together in a cooperative manner which benefited all three and ultimately those who harvested them. A number of maize kernels or seeds were placed in a mound of soil along with a few bean seeds. As the maize stalk began to grow, the bean plants would begin to wrap their own stalks around their partners and together they would reach for the sky. Once they were established, squash seeds would be planted at their base and as that sister grew, its leaves would shield the soil underneath all three helping to keep the ground moist and at the same time weed free. Not only did the Three Sisters grow in a symbiotic relationship, they also helped each other fight off pests and disease resulting in a healthy and plentiful harvest.

For Indigenous people, the way the three plants worked together for mutual benefit encapsuled their understanding of how everything on earth worked in a reciprocal, interdependent, and cyclical way. They honored their dependence on the plants through rituals and ceremonies, thanking them for giving of themselves so the humans might live and in return they were nurtured until harvest. Kernels of maize and seeds from the beans and squash were saved for planting in the spring when the cycle was renewed. European visitors to Indigenous fields commented on the remarkable size and health of the harvest compared to their own fields lined with row after row of one type of plant.[18] Plant scientists today are beginning to understand how different plants are able to work together to mutually benefit one another in the same cooperative and codependent manner.

It turns out that adopting horticulture was an adaptive necessity 1,000 years ago due once again to a fluctuation in the climate that lasted for approximately 500 years known as the *"Little Climatic Warming Period"*.[19] The warmer and to a certain extent drier climate put stress on the wild plants that traditionally sustained the population, especially those groups living away from coastal areas. The adaptation of maize cultivation in particular enabled inland communities to provide themselves with enough food to store for the winter months as evidenced by numerous underground storage pits dating to this period. Besides maize, beans, and squash, other plants were domesticated at this time; pumpkins, gourds, sunflowers, and the Jerusalem artichoke. Archaeological evidence also indicates that coastal settlements and villages were slower to adopt horticulture due to the abundant resources found in their environment, especially the marshes.[20]

Despite the importance of horticulture during the Woodland Period, the cycle of seasonal migrations continued as people continued to gather wild plants during the late spring, summer and early fall, hunt migrating water fowl and fish for anadromous fish during the spring, and hunt year-round. The practice of establishing task specific temporary camps that included rock shelters continued.[21] Festivals and rituals marked seasonal changes that focused on gratitude and a reminder that the people were part of nature and that its gifts must be recognized, thanked, and celebrated. The festivals were also a reminder that the community must always work to maintain the balance and harmony between the physical and spiritual worlds. Their survival depended upon it.

By the time of English colonization, the Indigenous people of Southern New England, like their ancestors, practiced a form of what is known today as spiritual ecology, a practice that links one's interaction with the environment with a deep sense of spiritual connection.[22] They saw themselves as not separate from the natural world but a part of it and related to all that existed in nature. This included a reverent, spiritual connection to the land where they lived and all it encompassed. Lucianne Lavin in her comprehensive study, *Connecticut's Indigenous Peoples,* quoted Schaghticoke Elder Trudie Lamb-Richmond who summed up the relationship her people have continued to have with the land and all things within it:

> *"Walking in harmony with the cycles of the seasons was a vital concept evolving from a specific way of life amongst Native American peoples of North America. They believed that they were part of the universe and all living things were relatives. They believed that it was important to maintain the balance of nature... sustaining that balance meant survival."* [23]

Chapter Four

The Disaster Begins

"Brothers, we must be one as the English are, or we shall all be destroyed. You know our fathers had plenty of deer and skins and our plains were full of game and turkeys, and our coves and rivers were full of fish. But, brothers, since the Englishmen have seized our country, they have cut down the grass with scythes, and the trees with axes. Their cows and horses eat up the grass, and their hogs spoil our bed of clams; and finally we shall starve to death."[1]

Miantonomo, Narragansett (1565-1643)

When Europeans began to arrive off the shores of Southern New England during the early 17th century, they found a landscape completely different than their European homelands. By that time, the evolving Indigenous population had settled into a network of villages along the coastal areas, rivers, and inland camp locations that were self-sustaining based upon their migrations that took advantage of the abundant resources each season offered. They were organized into semi-autonomous villages linked by affiliated family lineages that reflected their band and clan structures.

The first recorded European account of the coast of Connecticut and the interior via Connecticut River as far north as the city of Hartford, is the account of the Dutch captain Adrien Block. In 1614, Block mapped the shoreline and the river while identifying what he considered tribal territories. He described a verdant land that was well populated with villages surrounded by fields of maize dispersed within vast virgin forests. Sailing for the Dutch East India Company, Block mapped the area surrounding Long Island Sound east of the Hudson River where he had spent the winter in order to assess the economic possibilities for the company. His report was glowing. Soon after the Dutch company established a permanent presence at the mouth of the Hudson River on the island of Manhattan. From that point on, life for the Indigenous population of Southern New England would never be the same.

By the time Block had sailed into Long Island Sound, the people of the region would have been aware of Europeans who had been visiting the shores of Eastern New England since the late 16th century to fish for cod and occasionally land to trade for furs. There had even been a few attempts by the English to establish trading posts/settlements during the first decade of the 17th century on the coast of Maine and the island of Cuttyhunk off of Cape Cod. Both were quickly abandoned. Once the colony of Jamestown was established in 1607 in Virginia however, English ships returning to England often sailed along the New England coast, trading with the Indigenous peoples there and occasionally kidnaping individuals to be sold as slaves in Europe or the Caribbean. During the second and third decades of the 17th century, the Dutch began to trade with the people of coastal Connecticut more actively, collecting furs and cutting timber to be shipped back to Europe. They claimed ownership by right of discovery all the area from Cape Cod to Delaware Bay.

It is from the Dutch that the first historical record of the people who inhabited the coast of Connecticut and inland along the Connecticut River exists. They identified groups from west to east along the coast; the Wepawaug, Paugassett, Quinnipiac, Hammonasset, Nehantic, Pequot, and Mohegan people. Inland along the Connecticut River they recorded the Wangunk, Tunxis, Sicaogs, Poquonnock, Podunk, and others. Although the Dutch and later the English would describe and organize the population into what they termed tribes, they were in fact still loosely affiliated groups based upon location and kinship that had existed throughout the 3000 years of the Woodland Period. But as trade with the Dutch intensified, these groups began to coalesce into more identifiable political entities typified in particular by the Pequot who began to assert their domination over other groups beginning in the 1620's.

Although trade for European goods such as kettles, cloth, and other items the Indigenous people found useful were greatly desired, at first the Dutch presence did little to change the patterns of seasonal life that had always existed. But as Dutch demand for more beaver, otter, and other furs increased, competition between groups to satisfy that demand and obtain Dutch goods increased, leading to the destabilization of relationships that had long existed. Instances of conflict and violence began to increase between groups. Competition to trap fur bearing animals sought by the Dutch also resulted in their overexploitation which began the slide towards significant changes in the biodiversity and ecology of the region.

In order to cement their control of trade with the people of the region, the Dutch entered into an agreement with the Pequot to secure a supply of shell beads they produced called wampum. Wampum beads made from quahog and welk shells were highly prized by Indigenous people throughout the region and even as far west as the Great Lakes for their cultural significance. When strung together into belts, the beads were a sign of lineage, wealth, and relationship. The Dutch sought the wampum in order to trade with the Indigenous groups in the interior of New England and New York for furs. By then, the supply of furs in the 1630's was rapidly being depleted in Southern New England thus requiring the Dutch merchants to seek a new source of supply.

Although the Dutch established bases to trade with the people in Connecticut, at Indian Neck in Branford for instance, these bases were for the most part temporary. In 1632 however, pressure from the English expanding out of Massachusetts led them to build a permanent trading fort in the Hartford area on the Connecticut River. The plan was to capitalize on furs coming down the river from the north. By doing so, they further destabilized the already tenuous relations between Indigenous groups created by their presence and the earlier agreement they had made with the Pequot. The Pequot simultaneously sought to extend and solidify their domination over other Indigenous groups along the river and the coast. Soon added to this volatile situation was the arrival of English settlers into the Connecticut River Valley in the early 1630's.

Unlike the Dutch who came to New England to trade and bring the region into their global, capitalist trading network, the English came to settle and to do so required the acquisition of land. Earlier English traders such as Thomas Morton, who had a trading base in the 1620's north of Boston, had come to trade like the Dutch. The situation changed however when a group of English religious dissenters fleeing persecution at home, established a toehold at Plymouth on Massachusetts Bay in 1620, intending to stay. Forging an alliance with the local Wampanoag sachem Massasoit, they were able to hang on those early years with his help and then slowly began to expand the territory under their control in southeastern Massachusetts and Cape Cod. They were followed beginning in 1630 by thousands of English Puritans also fleeing persecution by the English King and Church who established the colony of Massachusetts Bay. An important reason why the arrival of both groups was met with little to no resistance was the fact that a few years earlier a devastating epidemic, probably smallpox, had decimated the Indigenous population along the coast of Massachusetts leaving large swaths of once inhabited land empty for the taking. By 1633, the English had their eyes set on the Connecticut River Valley where they were welcomed by the local groups who chafed under Pequot domination.

The arrival of the English to the shores of New England and then Connecticut was the start of a complex political, economic, social, cultural, and ecological disaster for the Indigenous people who had inhabited the region for 14,000 years. A dramatic transformation began almost immediately upon the English arrival along the Connecticut River with the establishment of permanent trading posts and then settlements. An absolutely catastrophic smallpox epidemic followed in 1633-34 that killed an estimated 50 to 80% of the Indigenous population leaving those who survived traumatized and desperate.

To make matters worse, disputes over control of trade, cultural differences, and disagreement over the killing of an English trader blossomed into war between the survivors of the dominant Pequot and the English from Massachusetts Bay in 1636. The English in Connecticut were quickly pulled into the conflict as the war engulfed the entire region. By the end of 1637, the English from the Connecticut settlements and Massachusetts Bay defeated the Pequot in a number of decimating, genocidal slaughters; first surrounding the Pequot fortified village at Mystic, setting it ablaze, and killing an estimated 400 to 800 men, women, and children. They then hunted down and killed many of the remaining Pequot as they fled in an attempt to seek refuge with the Dutch. Other Pequot were methodically sought out to be killed, sold into slavery, or given as prizes to English participants in the war and Indigenous allies. In the end the English achieved total domination over the surviving Indigenous people of Connecticut including their Indigenous allies such as the Mohegan, clearing the way for English settlement unimpeded by any opposition. The flood gates opened; colonists arrived overwhelming the surviving Indigenous population. With the arrival of thousands of colonists, the ecology and biodiversity of Connecticut and the region began the process of complete transformation.

The story of what happened to the Indigenous people of Connecticut following the Pequot War and subsequently over the next 400 plus years is a human tragedy that was repeated over and over again as the European-Americans spread westward across the continent to the Pacific Ocean. It is story of cultural marginalization, forced assimilation, and genocide. Adapting to changes to the climate and environment during 14,000 years, the Indigenous people of Connecticut had developed an evolving and successful series of cultures that emphasized humans as part of nature and therefore responsible to treat all living and non-living things with gratitude and respect. Their ability to survive and thrive for those thousands of years was a testament to their belief in the web of deep spiritual and physical connections with the Earth and all of nature. These beliefs would be severely challenged.

How did the English colonists view the environment of New England in those early years? When the first Dutch and English explorer/merchants commented about what they saw along the shores of New England, it was what they viewed as the resources that they identified and envied; the *"merchantable commodities"*.[2] Motivated by profit, the merchants who soon funded settlements in the new land did so for the financial opportunities they might generate. They saw every element within the ecosystem and environment as a separate commodity that was extractable and ready for the taking. One aspect within the environment in particular that overwhelmed those who first arrived was the shear abundance of the plant and animal life in New England compared to England and Europe. They were amazed by the numbers and varieties of fish from cod to those in the spawning runs of the rivers and streams. They marveled as well at the numbers of waterfowl and other types of birds including wild turkeys and clouds of passenger pigeons. In the forests and meadows the numbers of the many types of animals from deer to bears were beyond imagination. In their minds, they had truly arrived at an unspoiled land, a cornucopia of riches.[3]

There was one resource that immediately got the attention of the English colonizers; the limitless stands of old growth forests that stretched from the coast deep into the unknown interior. Coming from a European landscape devoid of trees due to deforestation that had continued since the Middle Ages, the sight of enormous oaks, hickories, beeches, chestnuts, and conifers immediately triggered the growth of timbering operations across the region that would not end until well into the 19th century. The result was a complete transformation of the ecology and biodiversity of Southern New England as the settlers reshaped the environment. From the outset during the first half of the 17th century, the colonists sought to recreate the landscape they had left behind in their homeland and with it create the types of ecological relationships they were familiar with. The wilderness had to be tamed.

In his book *Changes in the Land*, William Cronon describes how both the Indigenous people of New England and the English colonists interacted with and viewed the environment they initially shared.[4] He summarizes how the cultures operated from two completely different ways of relating to and utilizing the environment around them. With the marginalization of the Indigenous population during and after the 17th century, instead of living in a world where two different sets of relationships with the environment coexisted, the surviving Indigenous people were forced to inhabit that of the English. In a short period of time, the landscape of the region was dramatically transformed into a European one making the Indigenous way of life impossible to maintain.

As previously noted, the Indigenous relationship with their environment was based upon a spiritual link to all of nature and a belief in the interconnectedness of all living and non-living things in the world. Their culture revolved around their seasonal lifeways within the environment and a minimum impact on the surrounding ecosystem.[5] By using all the species of plants, animals, fish, and birds when they were most plentiful in season, they made sure none were overused. To do so, their villages were mobile in order to take advantage of the diversity of resources each season provided. As a result, families possessed only what was necessary and could carry on their seasonal rounds. By avoiding the acquisition of surplus property, they ensured their ability to move unencumbered while understanding the environment would provide them with what they needed.

This mobility and the lack of the desire to accumulate property or goods stunned the English who regarded Indigenous people as living like paupers in a land of plenty. They did not appreciate or understand how their successful relationship with the environment allowed them to thrive. On the other hand, the English way of life required the creation of permanent settlements that transformed the landscape by clearing the forests to create fields for their crops and pastures for their livestock. Underpinning this was the concept of land as private property which through its accumulation, prosperity was measured and assured. The colonist saw the Indigenous seasonal mobility as a sign that although they inhabited the land, by not improving it in the English manner, they were wasting the most valuable resource, the land itself. In their minds, by not properly using the land, the Indigenous people gave up the right to claim it as their own and therefore should forfeit it.[6]

In *Changes in the Land*, Cronon quotes the Englishman Thomas Morton who lived with and traded with the Indigenous people of Massachusetts in the 1620's. Morton understood how the Indigenous people thrived within the environment and admired them for that. Morton said:

"The leisurely abundance of Indian life suggested that there was something wrong with European notions of wealth: perhaps the English did not know true riches when they saw them".[7]

For this, other statements, and misdeeds in the eyes of the Puritan magistrates of Massachusetts Bay Colony, Morton was branded a heretic, arrested, and exiled back to England. There would be no stopping the march of progress as Pandora's Box was opened and the land was to be made and used in the way and image that best suited the English colonists. In Connecticut and elsewhere, the Indigenous survivors were pushed to the margins of English society and their way of life, beliefs, and understanding of the world all but destroyed.

Part Two

Ancient Lessons for a Modern World

Chapter Five

A Second Chance

"I know that our people possessed remarkable powers of concentration and abstraction, and I sometimes fancy that such nearness to nature as I have described keeps the spirit sensitive to impressions not commonly felt, and in touch with the unseen powers."[1]
Ohiyesa (Charles Eastman) Santee Dakota physician and author
(1858-1939)

With the coming of the English colonists in the 17th century, the ecology, biodiversity, and landscape of Southern New England began a massive transformation that has continued over the last 400 years and is accelerating today. Industrial and commercial development, population density, urban and suburban growth and sprawl, and rural fragmentation continue their march unabated towards what our society considers to be progress and a better future. We have become so dependent upon our belief system, world view, and material culture spawned by our creation that any possibility of moving in another direction seems impossible. We have created a culture and society that seems unwilling and incapable of making the types of changes necessary to live once again in harmony and balance with Nature and prevent the further degradation of the environment.

The story of the Indigenous people and their way of life over the past 14,000 years, as noted, was one of frequent adaptation to an environment and climate that fluctuated and changed numerous times. Their ability to adapt was key to their survival and ability to thrive in those evolving climatic and ecological conditions. Humanity has always been able to adapt to all types of environments and through our technology have proven ourselves to be highly capable of doing so. There is no evidence to contradict that clearly the climate across the planet has continuously changed over time through natural processes and will continue to in the future. The Earth as a living organism will always evolve and react to internal and external factors and changes; Continental Drift, volcanic activity, and variations in solar output for example have been important factors as our Living Earth is constantly changing. The difference now however is stark and startling. While climate and subsequent environmental changes in the past took place gradually over thousands of years that is not the case now. Climatic and environmental change caused by our human activities are taking place within a few short decades, not even the life span of one generation.

The complicating factor in the current situation and our ability to adapt or not to these rapid changes in the climate and environment is the shear scope of our dependence on the very elements that have and continue to create the global climate crisis. Our dependence on fossil fuels, our view of every aspect and thing in nature and the environment as a commodity to be exploited and profited from, and the unsustainable lifestyles we have created have launched us into a downward spiral from which it may be extremely hard to escape. To make matters worse, scientists acknowledge that unless there is a global catastrophe of unimaginable scale with a subsequent dramatic drop in the human population, a return to environmentally harmonious lifeways typified by the hunter/gatherer cultures present in Southern New England over the past 14,000 years is simply not an option. So what do we do?

We can listen to those who still carry in them the voices from the past. Although Indigenous cultures in North America and around the world have been subjected to repeated attempts at forced assimilation, cultural marginalization and disruption, and genocide, many have despite overwhelming odds, persevered and are rekindling and resurrecting their cultural heritage. First and foremost is their sense of connection to and interdependence with the natural world and the environment. It is their voices that we need to listen to.

As previously noted, Indigenous people as well as all of our ancestors dating back 100,000 years or more can collectively be called Animists by anthropologists. Animism is a general belief that all things within nature, not just humans, have a life force and consciousness. This includes animals, plants, rocks, geographical features such as mountains and rivers, and even storms. That life force or consciousness in the tradition of Western religions is identified as a soul and confined only to humans. This consciousness however, according to Animism, is present but different in animals and plants than in humans and it is no less vital and alive.[2]

For Indigenous cultures, this consciousness can be translated as spirit, but not in a Western sense. Spirit it is believed, is in everything, that everything comes from and returns to spirit, and that everything in the universe is made from spirit. Simply put, spirit is energy. Modern physics has proven that everything, including all matter is made up of energy and connected to and through a web of energy. They understand that physical matter is organized and held together by patterns of energy and these patterns are the reason everything is connected to and part of everything else through that energy web. Accordingly, although objects or things may appear to be separate, they are in effect interconnected through energy since every atom that makes up everything in the universe is connected to every other atom.[3]

Indigenous cultures, through this understanding of spirit energy, have always viewed life as an all-encompassing experience within this web of energy. This Animist understanding is not a religion but a way of life immersed in the experience of being part of the energy that makes up everything in the universe.[4] Through that spirit energy Indigenous people live within a natural connection to all life and nature rather than regarding themselves as exclusively separate from all that exists. Key to this experience is the knowledge that they are, along with everything else on the planet, connected to and part of the Earth (Mother Earth). This has always been and still is the natural state of being for humanity. The understanding that everything is alive and conscious through spirit energy means that everything then becomes a sacred manifestation of spirit and should be acknowledged and treated with honor and respect.

This system of understanding and knowledge is not simple nature worship. It is a vehicle by which it is possible to establish a two way communication with everything in the environment through this web of spirit energy.[5] This communication through spiritual energy with all of nature is an ability our ancestors understood and utilized naturally as a way of expressing their reverence and gratitude for nature's gifts as a form of reciprocity.[6] They understood that nature and the environment held the power of life and death and thus this communication was essential for survival. Observation with one's senses was key to this communication which opened our ancestors to a state of consciousness beyond an empirical understanding of reality.

Anthropologists have witnessed and studied Indigenous cultures from all corners of the Earth and have documented that they all, with little or no variation, live within this belief system despite the distances between them and complete isolation from one another. There is now little doubt that this wisdom and knowledge of the interconnectedness of every living and non-living thing through spirit energy is humanity's oldest understanding of how the universe works.[7] The pioneering anthropologist Michael Harner in his book *The Way of the Shaman* was one of the first Western anthropologists to study and research this wisdom system and its approach to the Living Earth extensively, bringing this Animist, natural world view to the United States and other Western countries. Harner and others have since identified this traditional Indigenous wisdom system as shamanic consciousness based upon its focus on spiritual energy and the ability of the practices inherent to it to connect through a state of spiritual consciousness with the rest of creation. The role of shamans in Indigenous cultures has always been to act as a vehicle of connection to the spiritual energy inherent in all aspects of creation, something that all individuals practiced and understood as a basis for all life. Harner describes this shamanic view of the Earth and everything on it as a form of spiritual ecology.[8]

Spiritual ecology is an emerging field in religion, conservation, environmentalism, and academia that recognizes the spiritual connections related to understanding that the Earth is a living organism and the interconnections between and interdependence of all animate and non-animate forms and elements. This growing movement, spurred by the rapid destabilization of the global climate, recognizes it has been our culture's overwhelming sense of separateness from the Earth and all creation that has caused the present ecological and climate dilemma. It seeks a reawakening in humanity before it is too late. In *Spiritual Ecology: The Cry of the Earth,* a collection of essays on spiritual ecology edited by Llewellyn Vaughan-Lee, Vaughan-Lee writes of our Western journey away from our connection to the Earth in the introduction:

"...we began a cycle that has left us with a world destitute of the sacred, in a way unthinkable to any indigenous people. The natural world and the people who carry its wisdom know that the created world and all of its many inhabitants are sacred and belong together. Our separation from the natural world may have given us the fruits of technology and science, but it has left us bereft of any instinctual connection to the spiritual dimension of life – the connection between our soul and the soul of the world, the knowing that we are all part of one living, spiritual being".[9]

As humans, we perceive reality the way we do based upon the parameters of the culture we live in. That has always been the most successful way individuals' function and survive within that reality. Thus what is accepted as ordinary reality is dominant within our consciousness. Hostility and prejudice against a non-scientific approach and understanding of reality has been paramount within our society. That condemnation of a consciousness based on spiritual energy and a shamanic understanding of reality implies a narrowness of consciousness that stymies a broader connection to creation and the world around us. If we are to overcome the crisis confronting us and all life on the planet, humanity must throw off our cultural blinders. We must return to an awareness and understanding that our ultimate survival depends upon our ability to embrace the Living Earth.

Brain science is starting to give us more insight as to how we perceive and construct the reality that surrounds us and interestingly it is proving what our ancestors and Indigenous people have always known. Neurologists and psychologists are exploring the role that the two hemispheres, the right and left, play in how we view the world and approach life on a daily basis. The British psychiatrist and researcher in neuroimaging, Iain McGilchrist has been one of the leaders in understanding how the right and left hemispheres interact and have historically shaped human perception of the world. In his extensive study, *The Master and His Emissary: The Divided Brain and the Making of the Western World*, McGilchrist looks deeply into how each hemisphere works to interpret the world it perceives as well as how they complement each other and work together to allow us to function in the reality of day-to-day life.

McGilchrist explains that in order for humans to function, the brain must be aware of and relate to the world in two completely different ways and the result is the creation of two different world views. In the right hemisphere, we experience a world of interdependence that is alive, highly complex, filled with unique beings and entities that are always in flux. This view is constantly forming then reforming a perception of the world that is broad and expansive and in which all is deeply connected. In the left hemisphere, we perceive our experience in special and specific ways; it interprets and relates to the world the right hemisphere presents to it by creating a version that is re-presented into isolated and separate entities grouped into categories on which attention can be focused and predictions made. Things become in his words, *"inert, mechanical, and lifeless"*. This ability allows us to understand things, to learn from them, and make useful things that enable us to function within everyday reality while giving us a sense of being a separate individual in control of all around us.[10]

Within the context of the environmental and climatic crisis we find ourselves confronting today, McGilchrist explores how it is the differences between how the hemispheres interpret and approach the world has in many ways created the crisis. He describes the important differences:

"The essential difference between the right hemisphere and the left hemisphere is that the right hemisphere pays attention to the Other, whatever it is that exists apart from ourselves, with which it sees itself in profound relation. It is deeply attracted to, and given life by, the relationship, the betweenness, that exists with this Other. By contrast, the left hemisphere pays attention to the virtual world that it created, which is self-consistent, but self-contained, ultimately disconnected from the Other, making it powerful, but ultimately only able to operate on, and to know, itself."[11]

According to McGilchrist, there have been various time periods throughout human history when one hemisphere or the other has been more dominant with important cultural consequences as a result in the development of Western Civilization. The

European Renaissance for example was a time shaped by the right hemisphere whereas the Industrial Revolution has been shaped by the dominance of the left.[12] Paul Francis, in discussing the role of the right and left hemispheres within human development in his first volume of a study of therapeutic shamanism, *The Shamanic Journey*, describes the differing roles the hemispheres have had in the evolution of humanity over the last 100,000 plus years. He outlines how Indigenous cultures do and our ancestors would have experienced life by embracing a shamanic consciousness that dwelt within a greater web of existence through the interconnection of everything that existed, a very right hemisphere approach which allowed them to see and experience the world as it really is. This allowed them to develop relationships with all of creation as part of it and not separate from it.[13]

Yet, in order to function within the world, our ancestors were and Indigenous cultures are simultaneously aware of both the surface reality, the world of the left hemisphere, and a deeper consciousness, the world of the right hemisphere. This was the natural state of humanity; one that embraced both a day-to-day consciousness and reality balanced by a deeper spiritual consciousness that connected them to the entire world around them.[14] In everyday life, the two hemispheres would have existed side by side enabling our ancestors to experience the world in a completely different and balanced way compared to how our current culture does. They would have had a sense of themselves as individuals while at the same time understanding and dwelling as part of a greater whole.

The right hemisphere allows an individual to connect with and be part of something greater; "*I*" becomes "*We*" according to Francis as it recognizes and embraces the "*Other*". It celebrates the wholeness, uses reason to appreciate that wholeness, and is consciousness characterized by empathy and connectedness. The left hemisphere on the other hand, according to both Francis and

McGilchrist, focuses on the separation of not just the individual, but all things. It views and experiences the world as "*I*" rather than "*We*".[15] The left hemisphere consciousness is self-centered, selfish, logical, rational, unempathetic and calculating.

During the last 6,000 years as environmental and climatic circumstances have changed, the left hemisphere has worked to give rise to the development of civilization as humans struggled to cope and adapt. Consequently, as the left hemisphere began to increasingly dominate, it began to shape a new consciousness that worked to suppress the right hemisphere and its sense of connection to and compassion for not just our fellow humans, but everything within the world around us; the animals, plants, and every aspect of creation. By becoming dominant, we became separate and the all-powerful shapers of our world.

As the climate in the Middle East began to rapidly warm and suffer from prolonged droughts 6,000 years ago, the population there increasingly depended upon agriculture and began to develop a culture that was city based, hierarchical, defensive, and aggressive.[16] The main objective of these early city-states and kingdoms that formed was the protection of their resources in an increasingly hostile environment, both ecological and human. This necessitated expansion in order to obtain more land and resources as a matter of survival. In order to construct and maintain this new reality, the left hemisphere began to dominate as it became necessary to categorize, separate, and systematically operate within a new consciousness that saw the "*Other*" as distinct and separate. This new consciousness suppressed the right hemisphere's sense of interconnectedness with not just fellow humans, but the rest of creation; the animals, plants, and the entire Earth. As these hierarchical societies evolved, they developed organized institutions that supported and maintained this new consciousness by creating governments, religions, armies, and social classes.

While these left hemisphere-oriented civilizations blossomed and evolved in various phases and cultural forms over the centuries in the Middle East and then Europe, they began to reshape the ecology and biodiversity of their environments through their separation from nature, turning every living and non-living part into a resource to be exploited for their benefit. The left hemisphere, through its ability to calculate, separate, categorize, and manipulate gave rise to a continuous stream of "improvements" to society through technological invention and institutional adjustments necessary to support and maintain the systems it created. In the process, this dominant left hemisphere consciousness put humanity on the track that has led to our current global environmental and climate crisis.[17]

The pace of left hemisphere domination quickened in Europe with the advent of the Scientific Revolution in the 16th century. By then Europe was also well on its way to developing a commodity driven, mercantilist, and capitalist economy; all very much the children of the left hemisphere. Based on objectivity, isolation of elements, logical, calculating, and factual, these systems propelled Europe and its Western offshoots forward at a dizzying pace leading to domination of the entire planet within a few short centuries. Other cultures across the globe in Asia, Africa, and the Americas could not match the technological power and organized aggressiveness of the European states as they sought new lands to exploit in order to obtain resources for their expanding market economies.

According to Iain McGilchrist, this separation became complete with the coming of the Industrial Revolution 200 plus year ago. This economic and cultural revolution came into existence by combining the advancements of the Scientific Revolution based on logic; rationalization, and compartmentalization, with the aggressive and self-interested drive of a capitalist economy. The Industrial Revolution unleashed forces inherent to the left hemisphere that were competitive, self-serving, self-confident, and unwavering in their sense of rightness and truth.[18] The result has been a dominant world view that does not necessarily value contextualization of consequences for its actions but views most issues and objects in isolation. This allowed for freedom of action in a self-serving manner by ignoring the ramifications beyond the specific needs and requirements of the specific goal. The sole purpose of clear-cutting a forest for example, became profit regardless of the devastating impact on the biodiversity of that complex, living environment. In doing so, the left hemisphere can easily justify such actions; the need for timber and profit supersedes any collateral damage to the environment.

Our culture has made tremendous material progress by embracing the all-powerful ideology of the infallibility of science and its fact based, mechanistic concept of the world. It has given birth to our modern era and its unswerving belief in the inevitability of progress based upon a sequential path of development and knowledge. This has resulted over the last two centuries in the technological and material advances that have impacted every aspect of human life while simultaneously executing the most audacious and self-serving assault on the natural world and environment. This assault has brought humanity and all life on the planet to the brink of catastrophe. In the embrace of the left hemisphere, we as a species, have suppressed and relegated the spiritual consciousness and sense of interconnectedness of the right hemisphere to a place on the margins of our existence. We no longer allow everything to be seen as the embodiment of changeability, impermanence, and interdependence within a greater, living whole. Our experience built upon interdependence of all that exists has been replaced by a sense of separation, isolation, and alienation.

Chapter Six

Shifting Perceptions

"Everything was possessed of personality, only differing from us in form. Knowledge was inherent in all things. The world was a library and its books were the stones, leaves, grass, brooks, and the birds and animals that shared, alike with us, the storms and blessings of the Earth."
Luther Standing Bear, Oglala Lakota (1868-1939)[1]

So how do we begin the transformation to experience a more harmonious view of the world we are part of, a view that is balanced between the requirements of practical daily living and a deeper consciousness that connects us with the Living Earth? It is here where the wisdom of our ancient ancestors and Indigenous people can guide us on the way to creating a rejuvenated sense of connection to live in harmony with the rest of the planet. It starts with developing a sense of place and belonging that goes beyond just being a resident of a particular location, city, state, or even nation. A deeper connection to one's surroundings and how we think about and interact with the environment can only come through a shift in consciousness.

Robin Wall Kimmerer is a decorated professor of environmental biology, a botanist, author, and a member of the Potawatomi Nation. In her work and writing, Kimmerer seeks to bring about an awareness of how we as humans can, through a marriage of traditional Indigenous teachings and modern science, realize our true connectiveness to everything within our environment. In *Braiding Sweetgrass: Indigenous Wisdom, Scientific Knowledge, and the Teachings of Plants*, Kimmerer details not only what we have lost in terms of our connection to the Earth from an Indigenous perspective, but how we can rekindle that long lost connection. In regard to regaining a sense of place, she presents one of the major problems traditional Indigenous elders have puzzled over since the arrival of Europeans to North America:

"They look at the toll on the land and say – the problem with these new people is they don't have both feet on the shore. One is still on the boat. They don't seem to know if they're staying or not."[2]

Stay or not. As Americans, we have always been a restless and rootless people, constantly on the move; historically westward and since the 20th and now 21st centuries, from town to town, city to city, and state to state. We are a people driven to search out better opportunities, landing often temporarily where those opportunities bring us. This rootless character only enhances our lack of connection with the environment where we happen to be. The climate, local weather, and any part of nature in the surroundings is at best only noticed if it inhibits or interferes with our daily activities. With our modern, advanced technology we have developed a homogeneous lifestyle regardless of the external factors where we happen to live. Geographical location and climate matter little unless sought after as a matter of preference.

Added to that sense of alienation from nature and the environment is the culture of sameness we have created through the mass franchising of the economy; same fast-food restaurants, same department stores, grocery stores, and the same strip malls have produced a sterile manmade landscape dominated by the familiar and comfortable. Moving from one urban or suburban sprawl to another is easy and although some places may have a glimmer of local character, they are overwhelmed by the sameness and as a culture, we seem to find comfort in that.

As a nation founded by immigrants, there has always been a sense, even after numerous generations, of being from someplace else, that we somehow carry in us a connection to a land we have never been to or maybe visited as a tourist on a family pilgrimage. This sense of "one foot on the shore and the other on the boat" has left us unable to see ourselves being of the place we are and identifying with it in a deeply connected way. Sure we can say "I am from New England" while settling in a new home in California because that was your place of birth though your parents may have been from Indiana and New York. Place is temporary and a consequence of chance, a rational choice, or preference.

Ian McGilchrist in *The Master and His Emissary* explains how the modern built environment in which we live and our culture are the product of the continuing triumph of the left hemisphere of our brains. Its rational, technical character and sense of separation has made it easy for us to remain detached from our surroundings. At the same time, the drive towards urbanization world-wide has propelled a greater and greater number of humans into sterile, man-made environments dominated by a sprawling maze of grids and paved surfaces that have exiled us from nature and the environment.[3] These man-made urban landscapes are designed to perpetuate mass market consumerism and the continued exploitation of resources that arrive from far-flung locations with detrimental effects on the global environment. We have goods from across the planet at our finger tips; toys, electronics, and clothing from Asia, tomatoes from Mexico, apples from Chile, and cars from Europe. It matters little where we live.

Under these circumstances one may very well develop a sense of place but that sense of place is grounded solely in a chosen cultural framework and almost certainly not from any connection to its ecology and biodiversity. The comforts of modern living have insulated us from our surroundings and the cost it is taking on the Living Earth. We are trapped within a system and frame of mind that seems paralyzed into perpetuating an unsustainable situation of our own making. What can we do?

As a culture and species we have two options. One is to continue on the path we are on hoping that somehow our technology and inventive wizardry will save us and maybe some of our fellow animal and plant species while adapting to a degraded planet and environment. The other is adopt the traditional consciousness and perception of our ancestors and Indigenous people in embracing a shamanic view by understanding and celebrating our connectiveness to the whole Living Earth. We can start by developing an awareness of how our actions and choices impact our environment, making sure they flow and align with nature in a positive way or are at worse, neutral. It is a simple start in the process of changing our relationship with the Earth and creating a sustainable future. This will entail changing how we relate to and experience the environment that surrounds us; not as separate things easily dismissed, exploited, or destroyed, but as *"family"*. Indigenous people since the time of the Paleo-Indians have always understood that humans, as just one part of nature are not separate from the rest, but believe all animate and non-animate beings on Earth are relatives; sharing the spirit energy and consciousness of the universe.

James David Audlin in his book *Circle of Life; Traditional Teachings of Native American Elders,* describes this Indigenous concept of *"family"* which he draws from the spiritual teachings of a diverse group of Indigenous elders including those of the Haudenosaunee (Iroquois), Tsalagi (Cherokee), and Lakota. Audlin writes:

"No matter where we go we are surrounded by members of our sacred family: the plant nations, the animal nations, the nations of the two leggeds, the spirit nations, the rock nations, the nations of lakes and rivers and swamps and deserts and forests and mountains. As family members do, they help us and we help them. Some help with their fruits or flesh. Some help us by providing useful materials. Some help us by providing great healing powers. Some afford us

protection. But all of them are made by the Great Mystery, all of them are therefore touched with the divine, all of them have a sacred message to teach us."[4]

Unlike our Western cultural tradition that has put humans on the top of the hierarchy of living organisms and the pinnacle of evolutionary development, traditional Indigenous cultures in North America still refer to our species as the *"younger brothers and sisters"* of all the plants and animals we share the planet with. They teach that the other beings have been in existence for a much longer time compared to the short period our species has existed and that we have always and still do have a great deal to learn from them, now more than ever.[5] By approaching the rest of creation in this way, everything that exists no longer becomes an *"it"* that is easily separated from everything else and exploited, but becomes a *"who"*. As a *"who"* they are recognized by us in a different way, as living beings and our relatives, connected through the great web of spirit energy. Our perception changes and we treat everything that exists differently; with reverence and respect in a reciprocal relationship.[6]

We all know that our way of life and the very existence of our culture, has evolved to depend on the entire global environment and all of nature for our survival. Everything our lives depend upon is taken initially from nature and the environment; food, materials for building, resources for manufacturing and transportation, medicines, and more. The list is endless. In this regard we are no different than the Paleo-Indians 14,000 years ago. But as our culture has evolved to this point, most of us are unaware of and completely removed from the sources of everything we depend on and consume and the destructive environmental impact of our consumption. By losing our connection to our *"relatives"*, we have lost our compassion and empathy for all our non-human relations. They have become simple commodities to be exploited for our benefit.

Our Western way of life has been what Paul Francis in *The Shamanic Journey* labels a *"taker"* culture adopting the term from Daniel Quinn who first used the label in his book *Ishmael, An Adventure of the Mind*.[7] The first taker cultures evolved with the development of agriculture in the Middle East, Asia, and the Americas when people were driven to accumulate a surplus harvest in order to survive and plant the next season, abandoning a more ecologically friendly hunter and gatherer lifeway. Over time these cultures became aggressive in their mindset in order to protect what they had and eliminate, if necessary, any perceived competition to obtain what they needed. When the age of European expansion and domination began 500 years ago, this system was perfected leading to the spread of the taker culture across the planet. Since the Industrial Revolution 200 years ago, the taker system has spread even more rapidly across the world and no corner has been immune from its reach and impact.

One result of the spread of the taker culture globally, propelled by the Scientific and Industrial Revolutions, has been our division of human time on the planet into two categories; prehistoric and uncivilized, and historic and civilized. Any culture deemed to fall within the uncivilized category is dismissed as primitive, superstitious, crude, barbaric, materially deficient, and irrelevant. Those that have managed to survive are dismissed as curious anachronisms of the past and of no importance. Their messages embodied in their cultural traditions and shamanic consciousness of interdependence are condemned as non-scientific and childish.

The Algonkian people of Eastern Canada and New England have a word for a consciousness and behavior like that found in taker cultures, dominated by the left hemisphere of the brain, and are highly destructive and motivated by selfishness, greed, and overconsumption; *"wetiko"*. It is understood to be a parasitic spirit or thought that motivates an individual to live a predatory lifestyle that aggressively consumes the life-force and energy of others for their own benefit. *"Wetiko"*, according to tradition is a *"virus"* of selfishness that infects a person or society. Paul Francis explains that wetiko can literally possess someone and once infected deludes them into believing that taking more than a fair share is a natural and admirable way to live without any regard for others. This leads to a selfish, self-centered perception of the world that lacks compassion or empathy for others.[8]

Indigenous tradition claims that when Europeans first arrived in North America the Algonkian speaking inhabitants immediately recognized the newcomers were infected by *"wetiko"* after observing their exploitive approach towards nature and the environment. This behavior was directly opposite of the beliefs and consciousness of the Indigenous people. They had and still live within a culture of reciprocity and gratitude towards all of creation knowing that the overexploitation of the gifts of nature would inevitably lead to their downfall; they were shocked and saddened by what they saw as a destructive and disrespectful attack on the environment and all of nature by the Europeans. Robin Wall Kimmerer notes that when she asked Potawatomi elders how people should approach nature for what they need to survive their answer was direct and straight forward.

"When I asked my elders about the ways our people lived in order to keep the world whole and healthy, I hear the mandate to take only what you need. But we human people... struggle with self-restraint."[9]

One of the major differences in consciousness between Indigenous cultures and the way we live is their important and powerful concept of gratitude. Their cultures, rooted in the concepts of gratitude and reciprocity follow an ancient understanding that besides only taking what is needed, one should also only take what is given. This dictates the relationship with all of nature since everything is understood to be alive in spirit energy and consciousness that must be respected and thanked. Important to this concept is the understanding that if we are to extinguish a life for the benefit of our own, then it must be done in a way that does justice to the life taken.[10] Traditionally dating back to the time of the Paleo-Indians, when taking a life by harvesting a plant or hunting an animal, permission must always be asked first. This shows respect for the plant or animal for what they are about to give; their life for yours.

This approach of only taking what is needed, only taking what is given, and asking permission creates an economy of sustainability that is best expressed in what Robin Wall Kimmerer describes in *Braiding Sweetgrass; Indigenous Wisdom, Scientific Knowledge, and the Teachings of Plants*. Sustainability has always been maintained by what is traditionally known as the *Honorable Harvest*. It outlines a respectful approach to what we humans need to survive which has maintained a balanced and harmonious relationship for Indigenous people for thousands of years. *The Honorable Harvest*:

- *Know the ways of the ones who take care of you so that you may take care of them.*
- *Introduce yourself so you may be accountable as the one asking to take a life.*
- *Ask permission before taking and abide by the answer.*
- *Never take the first or the last.*
- *Only take what you need.*
- *Only take what is given.*
- *Never take more than half, leave the rest for others.*
- *Harvest in a way that causes minimum harm.*
- *Use what you take respectfully and never waste any of what you have taken.*
- *Always share what you have taken.*
- *Give thanks for what you have been given.*

- *Leave a gift in reciprocity for what you have been given.*
- *Always sustain the ones who sustain you and the earth will last forever.*[11]

The *Honorable Harvest* operates on both a physical and spiritual level and only is successful when one truly understands that the taking of another life to support one's own must be done in a conscious way that recognizes and honors the other life as also a living being with its own life-force and spiritual energy; a being vested in spirit and consciousness. This consciousness embodied in the *Honorable Harvest* changes how all life is perceived and creates a profound effect that maintains a sense of connectivity and interdependence with everything within the environment.

Obviously, the great majority of people today will not be harvesting their own food but the *Honorable Harvest* can be applied when obtaining what we require to live on a daily basis. By becoming aware of the origin of the item or product and how it came to be possible for you to possess it creates a change in thinking that lends itself to following the *Honorable Harvest* guidelines. This awareness, if nothing else, begins to transform our relationship with everything we consume and begins to reign in our basic human tendency to overconsume.

It is easy to dismiss this traditional approach to consumption as naive and impractical in our highly complex system of acquisition of goods but it is possible, according to Kimmerer, to do so. The *Honorable Harvest*, for example, does not say do not take what is needed to live, but can be a model for what and how we should take what we require to live. We can take what is given with gratitude by consuming food that is harvested sustainably and respectfully, use technology that has a minimum impact on the environment, and celebrate the many gifts the Earth continues to grant us to sustain life; from the air we breathe, the water we need to survive, and the soil that produces our food. These gifts include the minerals we need to create our goods, and even the fossil fuels that have propelled our culture to this point of crisis. It has not been their fault we are in the position we are in, but our abusive over-exploitation of them that has led us to where we are today.[12]

The many sources of renewable energy can be harvested sustainably in line with the *Honorable Harvest* while doing much less harm to the environment; solar, wind, geo-thermal, and even the waves and tides of the oceans. They are all the primary sources of energy that have made life possible on Earth from the very beginning. By recognizing our responsibility to all life on the planet as well as future generations of our own species, we can in fact begin the process of adaptation that has always made it possible for we humans to survive. But change will only be possible if we are willing to adopt a different mindset, one that is rooted in gratitude, respect, and reciprocity.

In a letter to her eight-year-old granddaughter that appeared in an article titled *Algonquian Women and the Land: A Legacy* that was published in a collection of essays called *Rooted Like the Ash Trees;* Trudie Lamb-Richmond summarizes the change of mindset needed today. In the article, she describes the important role the Schaghticoke women of Connecticut have always played in maintaining a conscious connection to the land and the environment. She wrote:

> *"It is important for you to understand that our whole approach to the world around us is based on attitude: the way we view the world, the land, all living things. As part of the circle of Life, we believe we are not superior. As one great Indian spokesperson has said: "We are after all a mere part of Creation. We must consider to understand where we are; and we stand somewhere between the mountain and the ant." This is the attitude which prevails (and must continue to) amongst Indian people."*[13]

Lamb-Richmond continues to explain to her granddaughter

that every culture has its own way of viewing the world around them and it is reflected in the way they live. The Schaghticoke people she wrote, have always believed that each person must live in harmony with all living things and that they must strive to maintain a proper balance with the universe and all of nature. This is done through gratitude and recognizing the role all of creation plays in maintaining the balance and harmony of the world, Mother Earth and all its beings.[14]

We as a species and culture are quickly entering a fork in the road of our future existence that will determine our fate as well as that of the rest of life on the planet. Many prominent philosophers, biologists, physicists, and environmentalists are coming to the conclusion that the ancient understandings of our ancestors and Indigenous people about a living, interconnected Earth are in fact true. Visionary author, speaker, and educator Duane Elgin in his book *The Living Universe; Where are We? Who are We? Where are We Going?* describes the term *biophilia* first developed by the eminent biologist E.O. Wilson. Biophilia is our innate human urge and desire to affiliate our lives with other living things.[15] Through *biophilia* we instinctively feel a sense of connection and kinship with other life forms; animals, plants, places in nature we are drawn to. Rekindling this ancient consciousness and insight can transform our relationship with nature and the Living Earth, something our Paleo-Indian forebearers would certainly have understood.

Chapter Seven

Changing Consciousness

"Our original instructions are to listen to that cloud floating by and the wind blowing by. That's poetry and prose in English but it is "wakahan" in Lakota – it means to consciously apply mystery to everything – everything is alive and has its own consciousness."[1]
Tiokasin Ghosthorse, Lakota Sundancer

Imagine at this point we could have a conversation with some of our Paleo-Indian forebearers. What would they have to say after they got over the shock of not only the way we live but what has happened to the natural world and environment? What if anything would they recognize in this same physical place they once inhabited? What questions would they have for us and us for them?

Immediately noticeable to them in a dramatic way would be the changes in the landscape; how it is manicured and broken into sections by a patchwork system of roads and manmade structures that sprawl across all they can see. Some trees and plants they might recognize but most would be strange to them and they would be surprised and saddened by the absence of animal life and birds. They would be struck by the noises that surround us constantly; the machines and devices of every type that have become the background to our lives while remarking about the surprising silence of what is left of the natural world. Every aspect and element of our modern world and culture would seem alien to the extreme, confusing, and disorienting.

Since these Paleo-Indian visitors lived within a context of an interconnected, Living Earth where all that exists inhabit their shamanic consciousness and understanding, they would find it hard to comprehend how we can relish our individuality and celebrate our separateness from the rest of creation. Perhaps they would point out that is why we live in alienation from nature and abuse much of what is left. Our desire to reshape the environment to benefit ourselves regardless of the impact on the rest of our *"relations"* would be unthinkable and disturbing. When they ask us why, what would our answer be? How can we possibly explain that our culture has created and shaped this world to allow the fortunate among us to enjoy the highly technical and materialistic lifestyle we find eminently comfortable at the expense of many of our fellow humans and all the rest of the plant and animal species on the planet?

I am not sure if we try to explain that our way of life is based upon scientific logic and its factual application, our Paleo-Indian guests will understand. Regardless, they would more than likely ask what role a sense of shamanic consciousness plays in our understanding of the universe? When they ask whether we spoke to the few animals left around us, or the mountains or trees, what would be our answer; that we find that without factual basis, foolish, and superstitious nonsense? When they try to explain that everything on Earth communicates with everything else through spirit consciousness what would we say? They would be puzzled and saddened to hear that we talk only to ourselves; not to the rivers, wind, trees, or hawks. Our Paleo-Indian visitors would agree that we are practicing what Thomas Berry, as quoted in *Spiritual Ecology; the Cry of the Earth,* calls a type of *"spiritual autism"*, completely cut off from the spiritual energy of the universe and a consciousness that connects us to all that is animate and inanimate.[2]

The widely respected shamanic teacher, Sandra Ingerman, in her essay *Medicine for the Earth* in *Spiritual Ecology; the Cry of the Earth,* states that there is a practice in modern shamanism called *"deep listening"* that comes from many Indigenous traditions. According to Ingerman, we can always find answers from nature by paying attention and consciously listening to all of creation. Nature, she points out, is always sharing knowledge and teachings with us, as humans, we just need to be aware of what is being shared.[3] This conscious awareness played a key role in the lives of Indigenous people past and present since they were able to listen to and sense messages from nature that were critical to their survival; what the wind told them, the way the animals and birds reacted, what the trees whispered.

Current scientific research is beginning to agree that we humans are in fact not distinct and separated from the rest of the world but just as we act upon it, it also acts upon us. In our daily lives, we are influenced by the phenomena that surrounds us, whether it be the weather, geography, or elements within the surrounding ecology. Often benign, these phenomena can be beneficial like a soaking rain that ends a serious drought or dangerous and potentially harmful like a tornado or wild fire. It can take a form as simple as the shade under a tree on a hot day or the warmth of the sun on a cold one. This may seem simplistic but the fact that we are always under the influence of the environment around us is a simple reality our culture has chosen to ignore. We can ignore it but we are never divorced from it.

Scientists are beginning to understand and explore what Indigenous people have always known, that all life actually interacts with other life forms for mutual benefit. Just as the "Three Sisters", maize, beans, and squash of the Indigenous Woodland culture of New England worked together for the benefit of each other, plants, animals, and even we humans have always done so. It just seems in our sophisticated separateness we have forgotten. If the seeds are not planted, nurtured, and cared for, the plants will not grow. They sustain us if we sustain them.

According to Robin Wall Kimmerer, among others, Indigenous elders have always taught that plants such as trees actually "talk" to one another, something that plant biologists are coming to understand through research. It is clear now that trees, can communicate with each other by releasing pheromones which are hormone-like compounds that drift in the wind. If one tree is experiencing a biological attack, it will warn others to prepare to defend themselves by producing a defensive chemical. What is even more revealing in regard to plant communication is the role that fungi play in not just forming a reciprocal relationship with other plants, but in how they weave an integrated network that connects all the plants in an area via a type of underground internet. Although mushrooms that grow above ground are the part of fungi that we are most familiar with, the greatest part of their bodies are a mass of thin underground threads called mycelium that form an interconnected network that helps linked plants by sharing nutrients and information while warning of possible attacks by a toxic chemical.[4]

These mycelia interact within a reciprocal relationship with the roots of trees by providing nutrients and minerals like phosphorus and nitrogen from the soil while the tree roots provide needed carbohydrates to the fungi. According to Suzanne Simard of the University of British Colombia, neighboring trees, even of different species, also transfer carbon and other minerals between themselves via the mycelia. Research now shows that larger trees apparently help younger ones via the fungal network which helps seedlings specially to survive.[5] Simard's study has found that this complex network mimics human neural and social networks and that there are often *"mother trees"* that manage the flow of information through this network helping all connected to fight off disease and thrive together.[6]

Dr. Monica Gagliano of the University of Sydney in Australia has conducted ground breaking research into how plants communicate that aligns closely with Indigenous teachings. In an article published by the *New York Times* in August 2019, she described how her studies have shown how plants exhibit a type of intelligence and consciousness that allows them to remember, sense signals within their environment, and communicate. Dr. Gagliano believes that communication with plants is possible and has embraced the role shamanic consciousness can play in achieving that possibility while noting the pushback she has experienced from more conventional scientists in the field.[7] George David Haskell, in his book *The Song of Trees,* agrees that it is possible to hear trees "talk" if we can further understand their communication network. He also points out the important fact that humanity and all non-plant species have a reciprocal relationship with trees and need them in order to survive by producing the oxygen we breathe, absorbing the carbon dioxide we generate, and providing crucial building resources. Haskell calls trees

> "...biology's philosophers, dialoguing over the ages, and offering up quiet wisdom. We should listen because they know what they are talking about. Because they are not mobile, to thrive they must know their particular locus on the Earth far better than any wandering animal".[8]

Our Paleo-Indian visitors would agree. According to Indigenous and shamanic teachings, we all have the capacity within us to transform our consciousness and connect with the spirit energy within the environment by opening ourselves to deep listening according to Sandra Ingerman. So why don't we? In our current culture, it is one thing to imagine we can communicate with nature, that we can participate in a two-way dialogue of reciprocity and gratitude and another to shift our consciousness to embrace this concept despite the fact that our ancestors lived daily in that reality. Perhaps we can and it all starts with an awareness of our part we play in an integrated planet where every part has an impact on all others, realizing that we are not separate and isolated but an individual within the web of energy and existence, living within an integrated network like that found underground in the forest. We need to see the world and all it entails through a different lens to change our assumptions about the reality of life on the planet and our role in it. We must open our hearts and minds to be conscious of the impact our individual actions and culture have had and continue to have on the planet and all that exists. We must and can change our perspective. Albert Einstein said:

> "A human being is part of the whole called by us the universe, a part limited in time and space. We experience ourselves, our thoughts and feelings, as something separate from the rest, a kind of optical illusion of our own consciousness. This delusion is a kind of prison for us, restricting us to our personal desires and affection for a few persons nearest to us. Our task must be to free ourselves from this prison by widening our circle of understanding and compassion to embrace all living creatures and the whole of Nature in its beauty."[9]

Psychologists and cultural anthropologists understand that our culture and life circumstances shape how we perceive the world around us and form our reality. If these perceptions create our reality, is it possible for perceptions to change how we view our lives and the world around us? Psychologists agree it is and that it happens all the time. In this case however, what limits us is our culture's reluctance to perceive nature as anything other than purely physical. When we begin to perceive all of nature and the universe in a more conscious, spiritual, and connected manner our relationship with them changes; we perceive all of creation as sacred which alters how we relate to everything around us. The physical world and everything within the environment take on a spiritual significance and we begin to grasp that the welfare of all is interwoven with and inseparable from our own. Our ancestors knew this, the Indigenous people who have lived here for 14,000 years did as well, and those who are still among us do too.

Indigenous people have always seen their relationship with nature as one that maintains the balance and harmony within it through a conscientious understanding that just as the Earth nourishes them, they have a responsibility to nourish all living and non-living things that exist. This relationship was maintained through a conscious awareness, ceremonies, and rituals that recognized and linked them in a spiritual web of gratitude and respect. The idea that this reciprocal relationship might not exist was impossible for them to comprehend. The Haudenosaunee still maintain this relationship with nature and the planet through their teachings passed down through generations that see humans as a part of the web of life in which each and every part or *"being"* is uniquely valuable. Everything that exists, the sun, winds, mountains, rivers, animals and plants are respected and thanked in gratitude as connected spirits within a larger community of mutual aid.

The Haudenosaunee live as their ancestors did by what is called *"The Original Instructions"* which they say were passed down by their creator to the first people. It says:

"The Original Instructions direct that we who walk about on Earth are to express a great respect, an affection, and a gratitude toward all the spirits which create and support life. We give a greeting and thanksgiving to the many supporters of our own lives – the corn, beans, squash, the winds, the sun. When people cease to respect and express gratitude for these many things, then all life will be destroyed, and human life on this planet will come to an end."[10]

In *Braiding Sweetgrass; Indigenous Wisdom, Scientific Knowledge, and the Teachings of Plants*, Robin Wall Kimmerer describes how the Onondaga Nation, one of the six tribes that make up the Haudenosaunee, teach their children to start each day by reciting a *"Thanksgiving Address"*. Unlike our culture that celebrates a formal day of thanksgiving once a year, the Onondaga have integrated gratitude into their daily lives. It goes as follows:

> *"Today we have gathered and we look upon the faces around us we see that the cycles of life continue. We have been given the duty to live in balance and harmony with each other and all living things. So let us bring our minds together as one as we give greetings and thanks to each other. Now our minds are one."* [11]

The *Thanksgiving Address* then proceeds to express gratitude for Mother Earth, the waters, four winds, the seasons, and all the elements of surrounding life including all plants, animals, fish, birds, etc. From a young age Onondaga children grow up perceiving the world around them in a reciprocal, spiritual manner with gratitude. How different the world would be if we all had that opportunity. But it is not too late. We can change.

One way we can begin to change our perspective is to think of time in a different way. Joanna Macy and Chris Johnstone in their book *Active Hope; How to Face the Mess We're in without Going Crazy*, describe one method called *"deep time"* where as individuals we begin to look at our life and actions not within the scope of our own temporary existence but in the context of generations past and present. [12] They remark how during the Middle Ages for example, projects were begun which those involved knew would not be completed in their lifetimes such as the construction of a cathedral. But those involved took a longer view and understood what they were doing would have an important and lasting impact on future generations. It was more than a physical exercise in engineering and building, it was a spiritual effort that transcended time. A gift for the future.

Sadly, we are currently living in a culture that does not function with the long term in mind but instead operates through a dizzying series of short-term goals usually dictated by their monetary and immediate impact. Future planning is for the future to worry about and when it exists is often disjointed, fuzzy, and often resisted. When it comes to taking action in regard to the evolving environmental and climate crisis, the results have been a disaster. Indigenous people like the Haudenosaunee and the Algonkian people of New England have traditionally taken a different approach when coming together to make major decisions. They always ask, *"how will this affect the seventh generation?"* Because they look at life as a cycle of generations in which they are linked through time with their ancestors and descendants, they understand that what they do today will have consequences far into the future.

Thomas E. Mails in his fascinating account of his discussions with Fools Crow, the revered Lakota holy man, *Fools Crow, Wisdom and Power*, recorded the shamanic healer's thoughts on this and many other topics including his powerful and transformative healing powers and ability. Asked about time, Fools Crow explained that time was like a hoop in which the past, present, and future exist and all actions that occur are linked within the hoop. What happened in the past has shaped today and what we do now shapes the future. We cannot escape the cycle. Fools Crow said:

"Our children are us in the tomorrow of life. In them we remain here, and so it will be with their children's children – if the world survives."[13]

When we begin to become aware of the consequences our actions have on our children to the seventh generation, can we continue to operate as if what we are doing to the planet does not matter?

Fools Crow was the nephew of the famous late 19th century Sioux holy man Black Elk and learned the traditional ways and practices from his uncle and other shamanic teachers. Throughout his life, his people turned to him in times of physical or spiritual ailment. Beginning in 1974, Fools Crow asked the Lutheran minister and author Thomas Mails to preserve in writing the traditional knowledge and practices that had shaped his life and beliefs. Fools Crow died at the age of 99 in 1989. His teachings are more important now than ever as we face an uncertain future.

In his discussions with Mails, Fools Crow spoke of the relationship his people have with the Living Earth. He explained that a sense of unity and brotherhood brings about an awareness that expands to embrace all of creation so that each part becomes a living *"brother"* or *"sister"*. This awareness and consciousness results in the desire to embrace everything within the environment which he said was the *"core ingredient"* in creating harmony with the world.[14] Mails wrote how Fools Crow expressed this in his daily life:

"...his attitude about interconnectedness was another way in which he was given a deep sense of belonging, place, contentment, and peace... When asked how he focuses his mind on his relationship with the rest of creation he answered – Becoming."[15]

Fools Crow went on to explain how *"becoming"* works for his people and why it is so important. He began by telling how he would hold an object in his hand and through an open awareness and consciousness *"become"* it. If it were too large to hold, Fools Crow said he would hold it in his heart. Because everything in creation has spirit, all are alive with energy which can be connected with. He explained that the rocks, trees, water, and the ground we walk on are alive just as people, animals, birds, bugs, and all other creatures. They too have thoughts, feelings, concerns, and hopes. To become a rock, Fools Crow explained:

"I talk to it like I do a person, and let the rock talk to me. It tells me where it comes from, what it has seen, what it has heard, and what it feels. We become friends. When we are finished, I have a whole new picture of that rock. Doing this expands the way I behave

towards rocks and towards other things, and my mind grows. The more I do "becoming", the wiser I become about everything."[16]

After Thomas Mails had watched Fools Crow teach others how to *"become"*, he was convinced it actually worked. He began to introduce the concept to children to teach them the idea of and need to live in harmony with the rest of the Living Earth. Mails felt that if it can change their perspective, they might begin to see things differently. They claimed they did. Even adults claimed their perspectives were open to change.

When Fools Crow was asked his opinion of the current climate and environmental crisis, he was adamant and warned:

"Everything fulfills its role - ants, worms, vultures, wolves, pebbles, sand... when we damage any of these or the earth itself we damage ourselves. We cannot use them up or waste and destroy them without paying a terrible price for it. But people are doing this, and it is coming back on us all. Grandmother Earth is crying out about it. She is shaking the land (earthquakes) more and more to tell us how she feels, and to get our attention. Wakan-Tanka (the Creator) has told me that the Thunder Being will be sending great floods to show us the great cleansing that needs to go on within people. Our children will cry more than we will for this...their crying will be long and very loud."[17]

We have not heeded his warning and it has been clear the years since Fools Crow said these words that Grandmother Earth is indeed trying to get our attention and the Thunder Being has become a regular and destructive visitor. When will we pay attention? Can we shift our consciousness and change our perspective?

Chapter Eight

The Choice is Ours to Make

"When all the trees have been cut down,
When all the animals have been hunted,
When all the waters are polluted,
When all the air is unsafe to breathe,
Only then will you discover you cannot eat money."[1]
Cree Prophecy

Ancient wisdom tells us that we do have the ability to change how we perceive the world around us. If anything, the story of humanity is one of adaptability to changing circumstances. Starting 14,000 years ago, the people who first called Connecticut home experienced multiple periods of climatic change, some of which were dramatic, and because of their understanding of their relationship with the rest of nature, time and time again adapted and thrived. Granted, they often had the luxury of time to adapt as most of the climatic and environmental changes were relatively gradual unlike the situation confronting us today. Their hunter/gatherer cultures prospered because they lived in a spiritually conscious way within the context of the interdependence and connectedness of every part of the world around them. They approached nature with a willing sense of gratitude and reciprocity fully aware of the extent of their dependence upon the complex forces they were part of.

Clearly, returning to a hunter/gatherer lifestyle is completely out of the question and unnecessary. Rather, it is a matter of returning to the perspective and consciousness of all our ancestors that can begin a transformation of our relationship with the Living Earth. After all, if it were possible for all of us to trace our ancestry back in time far enough, we would find we are descendants of people who lived in a tribal culture that embraced a shamanic consciousness which considered everything within the environment as sacred. According to Tom Cowan, the important teacher and author of *Shamanism as a Spiritual Practice for Daily Life*, we all have a genetic memory we can tap into that can help us develop a renewed understanding of our deep relationship with all of creation.[2] We need to renew our vision of what is possible through reconnecting with the Living Earth and all its components.

So how do we start? When we begin to think about the enormity of the crisis facing all life on the planet it is easy to become disheartened and frustrated, thinking that as a single individual, we feel powerless to confront such an overwhelming situation. It is only human to feel uncertain as to how to begin the process of bringing about a shift in consciousness for ourselves let alone society. How can we as individuals make a difference? We can start by remembering we are not alone, that every day people just like us our coming to realize something has to change and an increasing number of individuals are making the simple choice of adopting a consciousness and vision that embraces the interdependence of everything on the planet. This is simply the rekindling of the essence of who we have always been as a species.

One of the greatest impediments to developing a shamanic consciousness is the collective cultural belief embraced by our society from its founding; the notion of individualism and the self-made man who by acting through self-interest, can build a successful life. This belief has been fundamental to the material progress and advancements made during the past 200 years and is a core element of our capitalist, consumer driven economy. It has led to the overexploitation of nature and the environment, many of our fellow humans, and the rest of the species on the planet. But now our extreme individualism has become a trap that is rapidly leading us into catastrophe. How can we escape?

One way is to realize that the idea that each of us is a separate island of self-interest functioning as an individual is in reality a myth. It has led us to believe things as they can go on forever without consequences for the next *"seven generations"* of our descendants, other species, and the Earth itself. We need to acknowledge that we owe our very existence to and are dependent upon not only one another, but all other organisms; the plants, animals, bacteria, and microbes. They provide us with everything we need to survive from the air we breathe, the food we eat, and even our health. Along with all the minerals we take from the Earth, every element within the Living Earth contributes to our wellbeing. Indigenous cultures have always known this and viewed the notion of interdependence as a key element within their vision of self-interest. If we begin to adopt the vision that the welfare of our fellow humans, all other species, and the Earth itself is in our self-interest, we can consciously transform how we live. Macy and Johnstone in *Active Hope; How to Face the Mess We're in without Going Crazy* advocate this transforming vision by explaining that a wider identity does not mean losing our individuality. Instead, it enhances it by expanding our consciousness to allow us to play a role and be part of something greater than ourselves.[3]

We have all experienced this sense of connection and interdependence throughout our lives both consciously and unconsciously and these many instances have brought us great joy and happiness as we embraced the beauty of those moments. It may have been with our fellow humans, a pet, or even a wild animal. It may have been while experiencing a beautiful sunset, watching the flight of geese, or enjoying a walk through a garden, park, or forest. There is something in our collective DNA that cherishes these experiences. Expanding our consciousness through a deeper awareness serves to magnify our connectiveness and elevates our fellowship with the Living Earth. A great way to begin is to follow the advice of Fools Crow and practice *"becoming"*. By consciously becoming aware of an oak tree, a deer, or a river by connecting to their spirit energy and *"listening"*, as Sandra Ingerman says, it is possible to gain a spiritual connection and a deeper understanding that completely changes our perspective.

Robin Wall Kimmerer quoted the Indigenous writer Greg Cajete in *Braiding Sweetgrass*:

Cajete said: *"…in the indigenous ways of knowing, we understand a thing only when we understand it with all four aspects of our being – mind, body, emotion, spirit"*.[4]

To do so is to completely change one's perspective beyond the self and creates an indelible link with an *"other"*. As studies of our brain hemispheres have shown, if we trust what our right hemisphere comprehends, a dramatically different perspective unfolds. When this happens, the world and all its parts are viewed as a living organism and not a series of separate entities ripe for exploitation. When we begin to see the Earth and its many interdependent parts in this way it becomes possible to start to view how our culture interacts with *"our relations"* in a different manner, one in which sustainability becomes a primary vision. We can move away from a cultural and economic landscape that views the Earth and all its parts as merely commodities to be exploited for our benefit. We can begin to practice the type of relationship with the Living Earth as embodied in the *Honorable Harvest*; if we *"…sustain the ones who sustain us, the Earth will last forever"*.[5] It is our choice.

According to Macy and Johnstone, our culture has an unfortunate way of dealing with things that are viewed as having a negative impact on us and society. When these negative occurrences take place, in order to protect ourselves we tend to ignore or avoid them in the hope they will somehow disappear and we can return to our life as usual. But we all know from personal experience, avoiding a problem only makes the situation worse and usually only makes the ability to deal with it more difficult.[6] When it comes to the climate crisis this is especially true on a personal and cultural level. In their book *Active Hope; How to Face the Mess We're in without Going Crazy*, Macy and Johnstone list seven ways people avoid facing a problem. Each defines a way in which many of us have been reacting to the climate crisis:

- *I don't believe it is that dangerous.*
- *It's not my role to sort this out.*
- *This threatens my commercial or political interests.*
- *It's so upsetting I prefer to not think about it.*
- *I feel paralyzed. I'm aware of the danger but don't know what to do.*
- *There is no point in doing anything since it won't make any difference.*[7]

The six reactions listed above have typified the many ways in which our culture has and is currently confronting the climate crisis. I can only imagine Paleo-Indian people reacting to the climate challenges they faced in the same manner. They would not have survived. Instead they adapted and thrived. They knew that their survival depended upon their ability to live in harmony with the world around them which meant understanding the challenges changes in their environment presented and confronted them accordingly. Is this something we are incapable of doing?

Susan Murphy in her essay, *The Koan of the Earth* in *Spiritual Ecology, The Cry of the Earth,* states what is the reality of this moment:

"From a position of accustomed comfort it is hard to conceive of living in a way that would require greater personal skill, effort, and

care to manifest the necessities of life. Breaking our reliance on the oil that has shown signs of peaking and beginning an inexorable decline, at exactly the time it has become woven into every detail of our lifestyle, is seemingly impossible to contemplate. The dream of an infinitely expandable planet placed entirely at our disposal was always just that, a dream, and it's fast becoming a nightmare."[8]

Can our society make the kinds of changes necessary to create a sustainable world where not just we humans thrive, but all life on the planet does as well? I believe it is possible. Increasing numbers of people are embracing a vision of a sustainable planet for themselves and future generations. The first step is acknowledging and recognizing what is happening to the climate and the environment is to become aware of the *"oneness"* of all life and the interconnected web of existence that is the Living Earth. We must become aware that the choices we make and what we do as individuals has a global impact. As Robin Wall Kimmerer points out:

"Our responsibility as human people is to find ways to enter into reciprocity with the more-than-human world. We can do so through gratitude, through ceremony, through land stewardship, science, art, and in everyday acts of practical reverence."[9]

Kimmerer goes on to explain that we need to restore our relationship with the Earth and all its parts:

"We need to restore honor to the way we live, so when we walk through the world we don't have to avert our eyes with shame, so we can hold our heads high and receive the respectful acknowledgement of the rest of Earth's beings."[10]

I believe we can. We just need to remember our perceptions create our reality. A shift in our consciousness can begin the process of changing our individual perception of what the world is. We can embrace the shamanic consciousness of our ancestors, of the Indigenous people who thrived in this place for 14,000 years. With this change in perception will come the hope we can leave for the "*seventh generation*" a world in which all of creation lives in harmony and balance, a verdant world where all species thrive, one we would be proud to call home. It can happen, it is up to us.

About the Author

James T. Powers is an historian, archaeologist, author, and retired teacher. He holds a BA and two MAs from Wesleyan University in Middletown, Ct. James is also a student of Celtic and Native American Shamanism. He and his wife Adriana live in a restored 18th century house in Durham, Connecticut.

Previous works by James include two non-fiction histories; *Saving the Farm; A Journey through Time, Place, and Redemption* (2013), and *Seeing the Past; Stories on the Trail of a Yankee Millwright* (2016). His latest nonfiction history, *On the Edge of Uncertainty; The Siege and Battles of Saybrook Fort during the Pequot War, 1636-1637* (2020) was written for the Old Saybrook Historical Society, Old Saybrook Connecticut through a grant from the United States Park Service, Battlefield Protection Program. It received a national Award of Excellence from the American Association for State and Local History. This summer (August, 2021), James' historical novel, *Shadows Over Dawnland* is scheduled for publication. *Shadows Over Dawnland* tells the tragic story of the first fifty years of interaction between English colonists and the Quinnipiac people of Southern New England during the 17th century and the impact that interaction had on the Quinnipiac and their way of life.

Thank you for purchasing *Modern Hope, Ancient Wisdom; Relearning Environmental Connectiveness*. My sincere wish is that it may help all of us change the way we consciously relate to and interact with the Living Earth for the sake of all life on the planet and the *"seven generations"* to come after us. If you have a moment, please feel free to add a review of the book on your favorite online site for feedback. Also, please visit my website http://authorjtpowers.com, to contact me, read recent blog posts, learn of upcoming projects and books, or leave a comment.

Thanks, James T. Powers

End Notes

Introduction: The Warning

1. Sun Bear, www.whitewolfpack.com/2011/08/native-american-quotes-about-mother.html.

2. Ofgang, Erik, Peering Into Our Environmental Future, (*Connecticut Magazine*, Vol. 83, No. 9, New Haven) p.19.

3. Climate Change, (Union of Concerned Scientists), ucsusa.org, 1992.

4. Climate Change, (*Union of Concerned Scientists*), ucsusa.org, March 30, 2020.

5. State of the Global Climate, (*World Meteorological Organization*). public.wmo.int/en/our-mandate/climate/wmo-statement-state-of global -climate., January 2020.

6. Green, Mathew, Scientists: Climate Change to Blame for Extreme Weather This Year, (*Huffington Post*, September 9, 2020). http://huffpost.com/entry/scientists-climate-change-to-blame-for-extreme-weather-this-year.

Chapter One: The First 5,000 Years

1. Black Elk, *Spiritual Ecology: The Cry of the Earth*, (Point Reyes, California: The Golden Sufi Center, 2019), p.89.

2. Bouchard, Michael, The Paleo Project: A Review and Interpretation of Paleo-Indian Site Distribution Patterns in Connecticut, (*Bulletin of the Archaeological Society of Connecticut*, Number 26, 2014), p.16.

3. Spiess, Arthur, Wilson, Deborah, Bradley, James W., Paleo-Indian Occupation in the New England-Maritimes Region: Beyond Cultural Ecology, Archaeology of Eastern North America, (*Journal of the Eastern States Archaeological Federation*, 1998), p.229.

4. Bouchard, p.19.

5. Spiess, p.246.

6. Spiess, p. 248.

Chapter Two: Adaptability and Survival

1. Chief Seattle, www.whitewolfpack.com/2011/08/native-american-quotes-about-mother.html
2. Bouchard, p.10.
3. Bouchard, p. 12.
4. Bouchard, p. 12.
5. Biello, David, What Thawed the Last Ice Age, (*Scientific American*, April 4, 2012), www.scientificamerican.com/article/what-thawed-the-last-ice-age. p.1-5.
6. Steffensen, Jorgen Peder, What caused the end of the ice age? (*Niels Bohr Institute*, October 10, 2020) www.nbi.ku.dk/english/scienceexplorer/earth_and_climate/golden_spike/video/spoergsmaal_svarl.
7. Lavin, Lucianne, *Connecticut's Indigenous Peoples*, (New Haven, Yale University Press, 2013), p.41.
8. Bouchard, p.12.
9. Lavin, p.40.
10. Lavin, p.42.
11. Lavin, p.49.
12. Lavin, p.42.
13. Bouchard, p.25.
14. Bouchard, p.25.

Chapter Three; The Archaic Transition

1. Sitting Bull, *Spiritual Ecology: The Cry of the Earth*, (Point Reyes, California: The Golden Sufi Center, 2019), p.12.
2. Bouchard, p.11.
3. Bouchard, p.23.
4. Lavin, p.81.
5. Jones, Brian D, The Middle Archaic Period in Connecticut: The View from Mashantucket, (*Bulletin of the Archaeological Society of Connecticut*, Vol. 62, 1999), p.119.

6. Lavin, p.84.
7. Lavin, p. 82
8. Lavin, p. 85.
9. Lavin, p. 121.
10. Lavin, p.90.
11. Lavin, p.97.
12. Lavin, p.130.
13. Lavin, p.144.
14. Lavin, p.135.
15. Lavin, p.157.
16. Lavin, p.174.
17. Lavin, .192.
18. Cronon, William, *Changes in the Land; Indians, Colonists, and the Ecology of New England,* (New York: Hill and Wang, 1984) p. 42.
19. Lavin, p.192.
20. Lavin, p.198.
21. Lavin, p.203.
22. Lavin, p.210.
23. Lavin, p.228.

Chapter Four: The Disaster Begins

1. Lavin, p.270.
2. Cronon, p.20.
3. Cronon, p.22.
4. Cronon, p.14.
5. Cronon, p.53.
6. Cronon, p.53.
7. Cronon, p.55.

Chapter Five: A Second Chance

1. Ohiyesa (Charles Eastman), Touch the Earth; A Self-portrait of Indian Existence, New York: Simon & Schuster, 1971), p.7.
2. Francis, Paul, *The Shamanic Journey; A Guide to Therapeutic*

Shamanism (Self-Published, 2017), p.3.

3. Francis, p.20.

4. Cowan, Tom, *Shamanism as a Spiritual Practice for Daily Life*, (Freedom, California: The Crossing Press, 1999), p.16.

5. Harner, Michael, *The Way of the Shaman*, (New York: Harper One, 1990) p. xv.

6. Kimmerer, Robin Wall, *Braiding Sweetgrass; Indigenous Wisdom, Scientific Knowledge, and the Teaching of Plants*, (Minneapolis, 2013), p. 31.

7. Francis, p.13.

8. Harner, p. xv.

9. Llewellyn, Vaughan-Lee, *Spiritual Ecology: The Cry of the Earth*, (Point Reyes, California: The Golden Sufi Center, 2019), p. vi.

10. McGilchrist, Ian, *The Master and His Emissary; The Divided Brain and the Making of the Western World*, (New Haven: Yale University Press, 2019), p. 31.

11. McGilchrist, p. 93.

12. McGilchrist, p.386.

13. Francis, p.13.

14. Francis, p.21.

15. Francis, p.110.

16. Francis, p.106.

17. McGilchrist, p.386.

18. McGilchrist, p.386.

Chapter Six: Shifting Perceptions

1. Luther Standing Bear, www.whitewolfpack.com/2011/08/native-american-quotes-about-mother.html

2. Kimmerer, p.207.

3. McGilchrist, p.387.

4. Audlin, James David (Distant Eagle), *Circle of Life; Traditional Teachings of Native American Elders*, (Santa Fe, New Mexico: Clear Light Publishing, 2005) p.9.

5. Kimmerer, p.346.
6. Kimmerer, p.183.
7. Francis, p.120.
8. Francis, p.127.
9. Kimmerer, p.184.
10. Kimmerer, p.177.
11. Kimmerer, p.183.
12. Kimmerer, p.180.
13. Lamb-Richmond, Trudie, Algonquian Women and the Land; A Legacy, *Rooted Like the Trees; New England Indians and the Land,* Carson, Richard, Editor, (Naugatuck, Ct.: Eagle Wing Press, 1987) p.7.
14. Lamb-Richard, p.7.
15. Elgin, Duane, *The Living Universe; Where Are We? Who Are We? Where Are We Going?* (San Francisco: Berrett-Koehler Publishing, 2009) p.10.

Chapter Seven: Changing Consciousness

1. Llewellyn, p.281.
2. Berry, Thomas, The World of Wonder, *Spiritual Ecology; The Cry of the Earth,* (Point Reyes, California: 2019), p.65.
3. Ingerman, Sandra, Medicine for the Earth, *Spiritual Ecology; The Cry of the Earth,* (Point Reyes, California: 2019), p.228.
4. Kimmerer, p.20.
5. Fleming, Nic, Plants Talk to Each Other Using an Internet of Fungus, (*BBC,* November 11, 2014), www.bbc.com/earth/story/20141111-plants-have-a-hidden-internet/. p.2.
6. Livni, Ephrat, A Biologist Believes that Trees Speak a Language We can Learn, (*Quartz: Whispering Pines,* November 3, 2017), http://qz.com/1116991/a-biologist-believes-that-trees-speak-a-language-we-can-learn/, p.3.
7. Shechet, Ellie, Do Plants Have Something to Say? (New York Times, August 26, 2019), http://www.nytimes.com/2019/08/26/style/can-plants-talk.html2019. p. 2.

8.   Livni, p.4.

9.   Cashford, Jules, Gaia & the Anima Mundi, *Spiritual Ecology; The Cry of the Earth*, (Point Reyes, California: 2019), p.204.

10. Macy, Joanna, Johnstone, Chris, *Active Hope; How to Face the Mess We're in without Going Crazy*, (Novato, California: 2012), p.50.

11. Kimmerer, p.107.

12. Macy, p.141.

13. Mails, Thomas E, *Fools Crow; Wisdom and Power*, (, San Francisco: Council Oaks Books, 2001) p.62.

14. Mails, p.63.

15. Mails, p.64.

16. Mails, p.64.

17. Mails, p.68.

Chapter Eight: The Choice is Ours to Make

1.   Cree Prophecy, www.indiancountrytoday.com/archive/13-quotes-that-remind-us-to-protect-mother-earth

2.   Cowan, p.13.

3.   Macy and Johnstone, p.92.

4.   Kimmerer, p.55.

5.   Kimmerer, p.183.

6.   Macy and Johnstone, p.68.

7.   Macy and Johnstone, p.60.

8.   Murphy, Susan, The Koan of the Earth, *Spiritual Ecology; The Cry of the Earth*, (Point Reyes, California: 2019), p.117.

9.   Kimmerer, p.190.

10. Kimmerer, p.195.

Bibliography

Audlin, James David (Distant Eagle). *Circle of Life; Traditional Teachings of Native American Elders*. Clear Light Publishing, Santa Fe, New Mexico, 2005.

Biello, David. *What Thawed the Last Ice Age*, Scientific American Aril 4,2012, www.scientificamerican.com/article/what-thawed-the-last-ice-age., p.1-5.

Berry Thomas. *The World of Wonder, Spiritual Ecology; The Cry of the Earth*. The Golden Sufi Center, Point Reyes, California. 2019.

Bouchard, Michael C. *The Paleo Project: A Review and Interpretation of Paleo-Indian Site Distribution Patterns in Connecticut*, Bulletin of the Archaeological Society of Connecticut, Number 76, 2014, p.5-32.

Cashford Jules. *Gaia & the Anima Mundi, Spiritual Ecology; The Cry of the Earth*. The Golden Sufi Center, Point Reyes, California. 2019.

Cowan, Tom. *Shamanism as a Spiritual Practice for Daily Life*. The Crossing Press, Freedom California. 1999.

Cronon, William. *Changes in the Land; Indians, Colonists, and the Ecology of New England*. Hill and Wang. New York. 1984.

Elgin, Duane. *The Living Universe; Where Are We? Who Are We? Where Are We Going?* Berrett-Koehler Publishing, San Francisco. 2009.

Fleming, Nic. *Plants Talk to Each Other Using an Internet of Fungus*. BBC. bbc.com/earth/story/20141111-plants-have-a hidden-internet/ 2014.

Francis, Paul. *The Shamanic Journey; A Guide to Therapeutic Shamanism*. Self-Published. 2017.

Green, Mathew. *Scientists: Climate Change to Blame for Extreme Weather This Year*. Huffington Post. http://huffpost.com/ entry/scientists-climate-change-to-blame-for-extreme-weather-this-year_n_5f5a26bbc5b628746bc193b1a. September 9, 2020.

Harner, Michael. *The Way of the Shaman*. Harper One, New York, 1990.

Haugen, Geneen Marie, *Imagining Earth, Spiritual Ecology; The Cry of the Earth*. The Golden Sufi Center, Point Reyes, California. 2019.

Indian Country Today, www.indiancountrytoday.com, www. indiancountrytoday.com/archive/13-quotes-that-remind-us-to-protect-mother-earth

Ingerman, Sandra. *Medicine for the Earth, Spiritual Ecology; The Cry of the Earth*. The Golden Sufi Center, Point Reyes, California. 2019.

Jones, Brian D. *The Middle Archaic Period in Connecticut: The View from Mashantucket*. Bulletin of the Archaeological Society of Connecticut, Volume 62, 1999.

Kimmerer, Robin Wall. *Braiding Sweetgrass; Indigenous Wisdom, Scientific Knowledge, and the Teaching of Plants*. Milkweed Editions, Minneapolis, 2013.

Lamb-Richmond, Trudie. *Algonquian Women and the Land; A Legacy, Rooted Like the Ash Trees; New England Indians and the Land*, Richard Carlson, ed. Eagle Wing Press, Naugatuck, CT. 1987.

Lavin, Lucianne. *Connecticut's Indigenous Peoples*. Yale University Press, New Haven, 2013.

Livni, Ephrat. *A Biologist Believes that Trees Speak a Language We can Learn*. Quartz; Whispering Pines, November 3, 2017, http://qz.com/1116991/a-biologist-believes-that-trees-speak-a language-we-can-learn/

Llewellyn, Vaughan-Lee. *Spiritual Ecology; The Cry of the Earth*. The Golden Sufi Center, Point Reyes, California. 2019.

Mails, Thomas E., Fools Crow; Wisdom and Power. Council Oaks Books, San Francisco, 2001.

Macy, Joanna., Johnstone, Chris. *Active Hope; How to Face the*

Mess We're in without Going Crazy. New World Library, Novato, California, 2012.

McLuhan, T.C., Editor, Touch the Earth; A Self-Portrait of Indian Existence. Simon & Schuster. New York. 1971.

McGilchrist, Ian. *The Master and His Emissary; The Divided Brain and the Making of the Western World*. Yale University Press. New Haven. 2019.

Murphy, Susan. *The Koan of the Earth, Spiritual Ecology; The Cry of the Earth*. The Golden Sufi Center, Point Reyes, California. 2019.

Ofgang, Erik. *Peering Into Our Environmental Future, Connecticut Magazine,* Vol.83, No.9. New Haven, Ct.

Shechet, Ellie. *Do Plants Have Something to Say?* The New York Times, August 26, 2019, http://www.nytimes.com/2019/08/26/style/can-plants-talk.html 2019.

Spiess, Arthur. Wilson, Deborah and Bradley, James W., *Paleo-Indian Occupation in the New England-Maritimes Region: Beyond Cultural Ecology, Archaeology of Eastern North America*, 1998, p. 201-264. Eastern States Archaeological Federation.

Steffensen, Jorgen Peder, *What caused the end of the ice age?* Niels Bohr Institute, www.nbi.ku.dk/english/scienceexplorer/earth_and_climate/golden_spike/video/spoergsmaal_svar1

Union of Concerned Scientists, Climate Change, ucsusa.org, 1992.

Union of Concerned Scientists, *Climate Change*. ucsusa.org, March 30, 2020.

White Wolf Pack.com. www.whitewolfpack.com/2011/08/native-american-quotes-about-mother.html

World Meteorological Organization, *State of the Global Climate, January 2020*. public.wmo.int/en/our-mandate/climate/wmo-statement-state-of-global climate.

Other books in the Earth Spirit series

Belonging to the Earth
Nature Spirituality in a Changing World
Julie Brett

978-1-78904-969-5 (Paperback)
978-1-78904-970-1 (ebook)

Confronting the Crisis
Essays and Meditations on Eco-Spirituality
David Sparenberg

978-1-78904-973-2 (Paperback)
978-1-78904-974-9 (ebook)

Eco-Spirituality and Human–Animal Relationships
Through an Ethical and Spiritual Lens
Mark Hawthorne

978-1-78535-248-5 (Paperback)
978-1-78535-249-2 (ebook)

Environmental Gardening
Think Global Act Local
Elen Sentier

978-1-78904-963-3 (Paperback)
978-1-78904-964-0 (ebook)

Healthy Planet
Global Meltdown or Global Healing
Fred Hageneder

978-1-78904-830-8 (Paperback)
978-1-78904-831-5 (ebook)

Honoring the Wild
Reclaiming Witchcraft and Environmental Activism
Irisanya Moon

978-1-78904-961-9 (Paperback)
978-1-78904-962-6 (ebook)

Saving Mother Ocean
We all need to help save the seas!
Steve Andrews

978-1-78904-965-7 (Paperback)
978-1-78904-966-4 (ebook)

The Circle of Life is Broken
An Eco-Spiritual Philosophy of the Climate Crisis
Brendan Myers

978-1-78904-977-0 (Paperback)
978-1-78904-978-7 (ebook)

MOON
BOOKS

PAGANISM & SHAMANISM

What is Paganism? A religion, a spirituality, an alternative
belief system, nature worship? You can find support for all these
definitions (and many more) in dictionaries, encyclopaedias, and
text books of religion, but subscribe to any one and the truth will
evade you. Above all Paganism is a creative pursuit, an encounter
with reality, an exploration of meaning and an expression of the
soul. Druids, Heathens, Wiccans and others, all contribute their
insights and literary riches to the Pagan tradition. Moon Books
invites you to begin or to deepen your own encounter, right here,
right now.
If you have enjoyed this book, why not tell other readers by
posting a review on your preferred book site.

Medicine for the Soul
The Complete Book of Shamanic Healing
Ross Heaven
All you will ever need to know about shamanic healing and how to become your own shaman...
Paperback: 978-1-78099-419-2 ebook: 978-1-78099-420-8

Shaman Pathways – The Druid Shaman
Exploring the Celtic Otherworld
Danu Forest
A practical guide to Celtic shamanism with exercises and techniques as well as traditional lore for exploring the Celtic Otherworld.
Paperback: 978-1-78099-615-8 ebook: 978-1-78099-616-5

Traditional Witchcraft for the Woods and Forests
A Witch's Guide to the Woodland with Guided Meditations and Pathworking
Mélusine Draco
A Witch's guide to walking alone in the woods, with guided meditations and pathworking.
Paperback: 978-1-84694-803-9 ebook: 978-1-84694-804-6

Wild Earth, Wild Soul
A Manual for an Ecstatic Culture
Bill Pfeiffer
Imagine a nature-based culture so alive and so connected, spreading like wildfire. This book is the first flame...
Paperback: 978-1-78099-187-0 ebook: 978-1-78099-188-7

Naming the Goddess
Trevor Greenfield
Naming the Goddess is written by over eighty adherents and scholars of Goddess and Goddess Spirituality.
Paperback: 978-1-78279-476-9 ebook: 978-1-78279-475-2

Shapeshifting into Higher Consciousness
Heal and Transform Yourself and Our World with Ancient Shamanic and Modern Methods
Llyn Roberts
Ancient and modern methods that you can use every day to transform yourself and make a positive difference in the world.
Paperback: 978-1-84694-843-5 ebook: 978-1-84694-844-2

Readers of ebooks can buy or view any of these bestsellers by clicking on the live link in the title. Most titles are published in paperback and as an ebook. Paperbacks are available in traditional bookshops. Both print and ebook formats are available online.

Find more titles and sign up to our readers' newsletter at
http://www.johnhuntpublishing.com/paganism
Follow us on Facebook at https://www.facebook.com/MoonBooks
and Twitter at https://twitter.com/MoonBooksJHP